The Art of Faith

the ART of FAITH

KATHY COFFEY

TWENTY THIRD 23rd
PUBLICATIONS

Dedication

For Dave

Cover illustration by Michael O'Neill McGrath, www.beestill.com.

Twenty-Third Publications
A Division of Bayard
One Montauk Avenue, Suite 200
New London, CT 06320
(860) 437-3012 or (800) 321-0411
www.23rdpublications.com

ISBN 978-1-58595-603-6
Library of Congress Catalog Card Number: 2006927963
Printed in the U.S.A.

Table of Contents

The Invitation

We are God's work of art. EPHESIANS 2:10

Welcome to an exciting adventure! You are about to take forty important "steps" in faith. These forty steps will deepen your appreciation of the beauty within you.

You may not usually see yourself as God's artwork. This book invites you to explore that possibility. It may seem like a stretch, but if you can see God as the principle architect of your life, it adds a marvelous dimension to your faith. So this book begins not only with invitation, but with prayer: that each of you, the readers, might come to appreciate the truth of the statement above from Ephesians. May everyone who follows the forty stepping stones of these chapters see how an authentic, faith-filled life is an artwork, permeated by the astounding grace of God.

One way to understand what this means is to look at the parallels between the divine artist and human artists. While those will be explored more fully in later chapters, or steps, let's say for now that both begin with raw materials. Sculptors start with clay. Writers play with words. Quilters choose fabrics. Creating human beings, God gathers particular genes, physical traits, talents, and personalities. Then, with mysterious skill and consummate care, God creates from these a person who is "unique in all the world."

The inner artist

When Karen Armstrong, author of *A History of God*, was interviewed by Sally Quinn of *The Washington Post*, she said, "Religion is very complicated. Some do it very well. Some do it badly. It's an art form." This then, is an invitation to do it well. It welcomes your "inner artist," who's itching to emerge. In your unique way, you can live and believe as artistically as the following two examples.

An Olympic ice skater who wants to win the gold medal must move from simply doing toe loops and triple axels to doing them artfully. To make the transition from a person on skates to fluid poetry, the skater infuses discipline, creativity, and grace, so skating becomes a symphony of motion.

So the faith-filled Christian transforms ordinary actions into spiritual acts. For example, consider the parent whose child is brutally murdered. The most natural thing in the world is wanting vengeance, pursuing the murderer to the electric chair. Yet some parents win the blue ribbon for forgiveness. They decide courageously that one murder doesn't justify another. They know that no capital punishment can restore the life of their child. Trusting God to bring justice, their gracious act of forgiveness reaches the level of art.

Seeing ourselves as God's ongoing artwork may help resolve a dilemma that haunts all humanity: the problem of evil and suffering. We can't accept a good/bad God. One God doles out hideous punishment. The other comforts and rewards. And yet, there is only one God.

We do not want to minimize the terrible dark, but we do want to understand its mystery. We do not dismiss the pain, but we try to understand its significance in the total picture. The experience of suffering adds a sharp clarity to an author's writing. So too our lives are enriched by the sum total of our experiences. Sometimes it takes real faith to look at certain aspects and say, "This isn't a mess. This has the makings of a Monet!"

MEANINGFUL QUESTIONS

So we must ask honest, meaningful questions about the sadness and joy God places within each life. Nothing is as disappointing as a spiritual writer or speaker who glosses over the tough issues or addresses them with a veneer of easy answers and cheap platitudes.

John's gospel honestly confronts the dark as well as the light, plunging immediately into the struggle between them. "The light shines in the darkness, and the darkness did not overcome it" (1:5). John's prologue begins with the darkness present in Jesus' life. If Jesus contended with evil forces, so will we. We may think of these as the four Ds: disputes, disease, despair, and death—with many variations on these themes.

The painter Caravaggio used a technique called "chiaroscuro" for the interplay of light and dark which makes up every life. We might notice the same thing on a path through a forest, where the dappling of shade makes fierce sunlight less relentless and the leaves' colors more brilliant. Just as the painter blended the luminous and the shadowy into something beautiful, so Jesus created an artful human life and invites us to do the same.

Jesus' own life wasn't a stroll through the rose garden. It spanned the full range of highs and lows. Had Jesus not known joking meals with his friends, wedding wine, weeping over Jerusalem or Lazarus, the thrill of catching fish, betrayal by a friend, and a tortuous death, he would not have experienced the fullness of human life.

When we see the beauty and meaning, the *artistry* in our lives, we do two things. First, we pause in awe to praise. Then we may start to re-order everything around this amazing vision: we are co-creating our lives, with God, as works of art.

RELEVANT QUOTES

Art is, after all, only a trace—like a footprint which shows that one has walked bravely and in great happiness.

—ROBERT HENRI

Not all are called to be artists in the specific sense of the term. Yet, as Genesis has it, all men and women are entrusted with the task of crafting their own life: in a certain sense, they are to make of it a work of art, a masterpiece.

—JOHN PAUL II, "LETTER TO ARTISTS"

PAUSE TO REFLECT

As God's work of art, we can all learn to draw! Consider the following reflections and share them with others, or make notes for yourself.

- What is the sadness in your life now? How have you healed from some wounds? Which ones still need healing?
- What gives you radiant joy? What prevents it?

YOUR THOUGHTS

_____

_____

_____

_____

_____

_____

The Foundations

It's impossible to build anything without a base. Metaphors of building found throughout Scripture echo this truth: a house built on sand will fall when the winds and rains come. Stepping stones will sink in mud without a base for this construction. The "building blocks" of specific arts will come later; let's begin with some foundation work. This book is built on certain assumptions:

1. Because we can't be the source of our own lives, we look to a creator outside ourselves.

2. Christians name this life force "God."

3. Into creation, God pours beauty, truth, and goodness, making all creation a work of art.

4. God leaves a personal stamp on us human beings, made as we are in God's image. God crafts this life with the same painstaking care and skill as God shaped the Rocky Mountains or carved the Atlantic Ocean. Thus, we become God's work of art.

5. Made in the Creator's image, the truest nature of the human being is creativity. All great art, made in partnership with God, speaks of God.

6. Two passageways lead into any religious system. One enters through its dogmas and doctrines. The other goes through its art, music, ritual, and literature. While both are necessary, this book follows the latter path.

The compelling nature of this approach became clear to me through work as an editor of religious education curriculum. We enrich our lectionary-based program with arts activities that support the Scriptures.

It's a delight to discover the painting, sculpture, music, and literature that enhance the Scriptures. As editors who had been through the lectionary cycles many times, our staff began to see familiar texts afresh. Religious professionals and regular churchgoers run a risk of overexposure, which robs them of wonder. The arts offset the danger by giving ways to step out of our routines and gain new insights on Scriptures we may take for granted.

The arts bypass tedious, academic explanations and invite the whole person's response. One child becomes absorbed in Salvador Dali's "Last Supper." A teen becomes fascinated by South African freedom songs. An adult finds sustenance in the poetry of Mary Oliver. The arts invite us to honor multiple learning styles and multicultural variety. "What do you see in the painting?" leads to "What do you think Jesus means by this parable?"

AND WHAT ABOUT YOU?

What would lead a reader to this approach? You may be in the mood to try something different. Maybe you're naturally drawn to the beauty and power of the arts. Maybe you're tired of churches being stern moral voices and want a more freeing approach to faith. Whatever draws you, use the same measure for this as you would for any work on spirituality: does it bring you closer to God? That, ultimately, is the destination of these stepping stones.

The faith-filled person trusts there is meaning in whatever they live through, whether it's joyful or sad. Elizabeth Ann Seton was widowed at twenty-nine and struggled to raise five children in the days before women had careers—or incomes. Two of her daughters died young; she saw her share of sadness. Yet she concluded, "I marvel not that I have lived, but that I have lived through it."

Some of our most gut-wrenching or exuberant experiences can't be verbalized. So to express intense feeling, we turn to image and symbol, the language of the arts and faith. They speak without words. Thus, they can touch our broken hearts and lead us beyond our isolation. Anyone who's seen the symbols in church—vine and branches, dove, flame, bread, cross—already knows the lingo. Jesus spoke it frequently: "I am the bread of life." The statement makes no sense on the literal level and in fact, scandalized his first hearers, who interpreted it as cannibalism. "Consider the flowers of the field" is an artistic—and more colorful—way to say "trust divine providence."

We can share the insights of artists, writers, and musicians who speak the language of symbol. Remember elderly King Lear, his mind unraveling, as he holds the dead body of his daughter Cordelia. He is partly responsible for the death of this one daughter who remained loyal to him. His poignant question has occurred in other words to every parent who has lost a child. "I might have saved her; now she's gone for ever....Why should a dog, a horse, a rat have life, /And thou no breath at all?" Tragic ordeal transformed to poetry: this is the model for any faithful life.

As you begin this book, see each chapter as a stepping stone. Just as Jesus focused on the process ("I am the way"), so should we. These thoughts and activities may not lead to a dramatic end. They may mark only the beginning of a lifelong quest. No work on spirituality would be complete without its ancient Chinese proverb. The one most fitting for this book says: the bird doesn't sing because it has an answer; the bird sings because it has a song.

RELEVANT QUOTES

You must build your life as if it were a work of art.
—ABRAHAM HESCHEL

In art, either as creators or participators, we are helped to remember some of the glorious things we have forgotten, and some of the terrible things we are asked to endure, we who are children of God by adoption and grace.
—MADELEINE L'ENGLE, *Walking on Water*
(NEW YORK: NORTH POINT PRESS, 1980, 19)

Creativity means making something for the soul out of every experience.
—THOMAS MOORE

Everything you do is focused upon the creative process—whether you are picking a flower, hiking, or preparing a meal.
—DEENA METZGER

PAUSE TO REFLECT

- Take stock as you begin. What draws you to exploring your life as God's work of art? What are your reservations? After your initial response, leave space here so you can add to your thoughts as you progress.

step 3

The Art of Imitation

The Lord created me at the beginning of his work,
*   the first of his acts of long ago.*
Before the mountains had been shaped,
*   before the hills, I was brought forth....*
When he established the heavens, I was there...
*   then I was beside him, like a master worker;*
*   and I was daily his delight,*
*   rejoicing before him always,*
Rejoicing in his inhabited world
*   and delighting in the human race.* PROVERBS 8:22, 25, 27, 30–31

It's time to take the third important step. The biblical passage above shows God and human engaged together in the same delightful creativity. An interesting footnote to "like a master worker" in the NRSV translation says "like a little child." Perhaps the two aren't so different. They are equally fearless, totally absorbed, and thoroughly given over to delight.

Just as the baker gives his child a small ball of dough or a potter gives her child a lump of clay, so the child happily does the same work on a lesser scale. Latina cooks learn to make tortillas beside a

9

mother or grandmother who weighs the ingredients in her hands and teaches them by example how to shape the perfect circle. In European museums, apprentices often cluster in front of master-pieces, learning to paint through imitation. So we, in a specific art or an artful life, imitate the work of God. Our happiness springs from God's presence beside us, our parallel activity.

Several elements are common to both God's work and ours:

- loving care
- discipline or order
- playfulness or surprise
- reverence: everything matters
- inspiration: recognizing that all is given
- sensitivity to the grace notes, the transcendent dimension.

Sometimes the arts reach a peak of perfection in a Beethoven symphony, a Shakespearean sonnet, a Shaker chair, or a Michelangelo sculpture. We call them "inspired" because they contain a glimpse of God's self-revelation.

WE BELIEVE

Christians believe that Jesus is our "way, truth, and life." Only by imitating him can we achieve the fullness of human life. And how did Jesus live?

- With eyes fixed on his loving father, source of ultimate good-ness and beauty which sustained him daily.
- With some disregard for the "rules" of his day, like not curing or not picking grain on the Sabbath.
- With an immense appreciation for the world around him: a cascade of silvery fish into a boat, the silky feel of ointment on his feet, birdsong, vines, stalks of wheat.
- With an imagination that could recognize the poverty and disease surrounding him like an odor, yet still call the people before him "blessed."

"But," some may protest. "Isn't faith a more dogged matter of keeping rules and attending religious services?" There's nothing wrong with that.

Approaching faith through the arts provides us a different way to see. In his book *A Wounded Innocence*, Alejandro Garcia-Rivera made a distinction between "textbook theology" and "living theology" which touches our hearts because it uses story, image, and song (Collegeville, MN: The Liturgical Press, 2003, viii).

If we have inherited a treasure in our faith, as we say we believe, then why do we live like paupers? If we have such a short time on earth, why do we squander it? Let's paint, as beautifully as we can, the canvas of our lives.

PRAYER

Creator God,
It's hard to see my work as play.
I tend to take myself so seriously!
But playing beside you makes all the difference.
Come, let us create the masterpiece of a life together.

SCRIPTURE

Read the story of the Samaritan woman collaborating with Jesus in the work of harvest (John 4:39–42). Focus initially on her role. She must've been persuasive (maybe it was the costly vulnerability of admitting "he told me everything I ever did" [v. 39]). Whatever she said to her neighbors was effective. Somehow she invited the Samaritans to move beyond their cultural taboo of not sharing dishes with a Jew, and asking Jesus to stay with them.

RELEVANT QUOTES

What has been said to me? How has my life replied?

—DENISE LEVERTOV

I do believe it is possible to create, even without writing a word or painting a picture, by simply molding one's inner life.

—Etty Hillesum

Everyone is an artist in charge of designing his or her life.

—Frances E. Vaughan

Christianity and art had a long and spectacularly successful marriage. Their offspring are everywhere.

—Michael J. Farrell

Pause to reflect

- What difference might it make in your daily outlook if you regarded yourself as working beside God, playing at God's side, delighting in each other?

Your thoughts

_____

_____

_____

_____

_____

_____

_____

Intersections: Art & Faith

Drums thrumming, clarinets and trombones blaring brassily, the Queen City Jazz Band marches around the perimeter of the round church. Stained glass glints in the same coppery tones as the trumpets. The audience claps and sizzles along with the smoky New Orleans Jazz. The altar has been moved aside and the raised platform becomes a stage for the banjo player and booming voice of the soloist singing "All God's Critters Got a Place in the Choir." When the band exits to "When the Saints Go Marching In," everyone sings along and some can't help dancing.

A photo exhibit lines the corridor to the retreat center chapel. Regular visitors look eagerly for the newest work of the resident Jesuit photographer. This summer, it's photos from the spring season. A tightly curled, hot pink bud seems poised on the brink of bursting into bloom. In another, an explosion of ivory apple blossoms drifts across a cloudless, china blue sky. The spring passed too quickly for some of us to appreciate it, but here it is frozen in time and framed, awaiting our grateful response.

The choir surrounds the audience and booms out the "Hallelujah Chorus" from Handel's *Messiah*. Seeing Rembrandt's paintings of the Prodigal Son, the Nativity, or the Raising of Lazarus gives people a new lens on the familiar gospel stories.

The arts and faith are a match made in heaven—and always have been. For centuries, the church has taught faith through the arts. In Western Christian art, the stained glass windows of a Gothic cathedral made a belief system accessible to the illiterate. Medieval theologians named religious art a *porta coeli*, or "gate of heaven," through which God touched human beings and humans expressed their longing for God.

BEAUTY INSPIRES

Abbot Suger of St. Denis in France faced stiff opposition when he undertook the remodeling of the abbey chapel. Bernard of Clairvaux, champion of monastic reform, called for austerity and criticized Suger's commissioning of beautiful stained glass windows. But as Alejandro Garcia-Rivera points out in *A Wounded Innocence*, "he did theology of art a great favor. He forced Suger to articulate a theology of art to counter his critique. In other words, Bernard forced Suger to give spiritual justification for bringing beauty into a place meant for the mortification of one's soul" (64).

Suger rose to the challenge. He wrote that in entering a lovely place, he received the grace to see himself dwelling in "some strange region of the universe which neither exists entirely in the slime of the earth nor entirely in the purity of Heaven."

So Abbot Suger had his craftspeople frame the doorway to the church with an invitation to pilgrims. It told them they were entering a place that hovers "between the world to come and the world that is." The twilight blue from the windows continues to inspire those who find themselves somewhere between the woundedness of this world and the bright hope of the next. It is meant to give us a sense of "Heaven-with-us" and at the same time, a compassion for the suffering of this world.

MUSIC, TOO

The film *The Mission* begins with an exquisitely beautiful solo called "Gabriel's Oboe." It is played by a young Jesuit coming to South America to establish missions there. The voice-over comments wryly, "With an orchestra, the Jesuits could have subdued the continent."

The missionaries worked with the talents of the Guarani to create magnificent choirs, build musical instruments, and channel native abilities into worship. Political feuds eventually destroyed these centers which blended art and faith. But the movie's final scenes show one of the indigenous leaders rescuing the monstrance and carrying it when the priest is shot and falls. In another, a little girl retrieves a violin from the wreckage—a hopeful symbol that the best of the tradition survives.

So the contemporary scenes mentioned in the first three paragraphs of this chapter aren't revolutionary, but continue a long tradition. Ways of teaching the faith that rely heavily on traditional teaching may give way to learning through delight. A survey conducted by *US Catholic* magazine of 140 readers revealed the following:

- 96% agreed that art could bring them closer to God.
- 95% agreed that art didn't need to be religious to bring them closer to God.
- 76% believed the church should do more to encourage artists to create religious art. (Maureen Abood, "How Great Thou Art," January 2004, 28–30)

In *Radical Optimism,* Beatrice Bruteau makes the connection between our sacramental tradition and the art of living:

Take pleasure in everything you do....Whatever we do should be just like our sacramental experiences. After all, the sacraments are there to teach us how to have daily experiences, daily bread, daily...nourishing experiences. And daily wine that rejoices our hearts. It is not only when one is before the altar that one can feel this joy. It can be experienced when we are doing whatever trivial or tedious task is the work of the moment. You've put on your alb (or apron) and taken candle (or pot) in hand, and you're going to the altar (or sink). Whatever you're doing it is worship, it is divine expression, and it is joy. (New York: Crossroad, 1996, 132)

RELEVANT QUOTES

Art washes away from the soul the dust of everyday life.

—PABLO PICASSO

Music and art and poetry attune the soul to God.

—THOMAS MERTON

PAUSE TO REFLECT

- To which of the arts are you most drawn? Music? Painting or sculpture? Literature? Another? Why does it touch you?

God's Artistry

*In the beginning when God created the heavens and the earth, the
earth was a formless void and darkness covered the face of the
deep....God said, "Let there be light"; and there was light. And God
saw that the light was good; and God separated the light from the
darkness. God called the light Day, and the darkness he called Night.*

*God saw everything that he had made, and indeed, it was very
good.* GENESIS 1:1–5, 31

The fifth step invites us to consider the nature of God's Self. One
task of a healthy, mature spirituality is to broaden our images of
God. Some need to move beyond the punitive God, who records
every misdeed and extracts a terrible vengeance. For others, their
images of God have grown stale and flat, failing to give life.

All these—and many others—may find new life in the image of
God as creator, pouring infinite energy into beloved creatures and
creation. Throughout Scripture, God is artist, swirling waters and
pouring light in Genesis, creating and animating a people, taking
infinite care to preserve the Hebrews from harm.

Maybe we've grown overly solemn about the creation story. We
forget God's gumption, the wild abandon of the first sunset in

Calypso colors or the exultation at the first streak of cheetah through rainforest. The greatest understatement ever must be the refrain throughout Genesis: "And God saw that it was good." But that restraint allows us room to imagine. Maybe God really said, "Whee! A waterfall! A crystal cascade—and a bodacious splash!"

ATTENTION TO DETAIL

Anyone who has ever watched an artist work notices the keen attention to detail. He or she will spend hours on something that may seem insignificant to the untrained eye or ear: capturing the precise color tone for this cloud, honing the word choices for that poem, endlessly practicing the notes of a concerto so they flow together seamlessly.

If this is true for the human artist, so it must be for God. In Genesis, God pauses daily to delight, much like a freckled eight year old squealing deliciously at creepy-crawly things. When we observe how light falls on almost-transparent petals or how waves trace scallops in sand, we participate in God's delight.

JESUS: THE ULTIMATE ARTIST

When God became human as Jesus, he was the most creative person who ever lived. That may help explain why Jesus has inspired lives of artistry and sacrifice, and why he continues to appeal and challenge centuries after he lived. His stories intrigue listeners even today because they rarely end predictably, consistently upset the apple cart, and sneak in a profound teaching when listeners aren't looking.

Jesus' cures restore God's first dream for a person to be whole and beautiful. He wants a woman to stand erect, not bent over. He invites the blind to see and tells a paralytic to take up his mat and walk home. He restores a dead man to his grieving mother and a little girl to her parents. He carries before him a vision of what God intended, and takes action to make that happen.

His creative powers bring life even to the wreckage. Lazarus rises. Jesus' own tomb is empty. People gradually recover from cancer, divorce, abuse, loss of homes, limbs, and loved ones. Jesus blows on the spark of life glowing in the embers and kindles flame from the ashes.

Sometimes, it's comforting to know that we are still works-in-progress. Just as a book often carries a working title until its themes emerge fully, so too we gradually find our way to our deepest truths. Surely one of these is our ability to mirror God's creativity, its human form in Jesus.

RELEVANT QUOTE

Looking at God's creation, it is pretty clear that the creator did not know when to stop. There is not one pink flower, or even fifty pink flowers, but hundreds. Snowflakes, of course, are the ultimate exercise in sheer creative glee. No two alike. This creator looks suspiciously like someone who just might send us support for our creative ventures. —JULIA CAMERON

PAUSE TO REFLECT

- Think about the marvels of creation and the refrain "it was good." What would you particularly like to compliment? Create words of praise.

- Complete this sentence every day for a week: "God, today you did an especially fine job on…." Some possible answers: the scent of orange blossom, the chiseled icicle hanging by the garage, the helpful clerk at the store, the taste of a ripe pear, the wind ruffling leaves, the shiny purple skin of eggplant, a lopsided grin.

step 6

The Grand Design

O Lord, our Sovereign,
How majestic is your name in all the earth!
When I look at your heavens, the work of your fingers,
the moon and the stars that you have established;
what are human beings that you are mindful of them,
mortals that you care for them?
Yet you have made them a little lower than God,
and crowned them with glory and honor. PSALM 8:1, 3–5

Every great work of art needs both the big vision and the tiny details, so steps six and step seven go together.

Where we stand in a larger scheme might be represented as a series of arches that began long before our births and continue into an eternity long past our time on earth. No artist, composer, novelist, or poet stands in isolation. They may continue parts of their tradition or break with it, but somehow they're influenced by those who came before—and plant seeds for those who follow. So too for the person of faith. We stand squarely planted in a long line of believers, some who came before, others who follow us.

To get a concrete metaphor for one's faith life as a work of art, picture an arch. Perhaps you've seen the Eero Saarinen arch, a gleaming, silver, 630-foot "Gateway to the West" rising from the St. Louis riverfront. A local cathedral or church may have Gothic arches that support the weight of soaring ceilings so the walls can hold stained glass. Many cloisters, like the museum in New York or the California monasteries, have a series of beautiful arches.

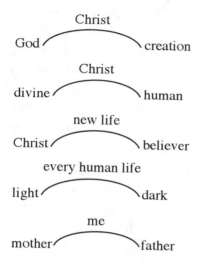

Now that you have the arch shape in mind, think of a series of arches that stretch back to the beginning of time and up to the present moment.

During baptisms at our parish we sing David Haas's song, "This Child of Yours." It creates another arch, and each of us could write our names across the intersection at the top:

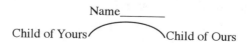

In every human being, divine joins human, just as Jesus is the human face of God. God is parent, co-creating with human parents.

We could compare the work of a novelist plotting a story to God's grand design. John Irving explains that he never writes the first sentence until he knows exactly what will happen at the end. "Because I don't start a novel until I know the ending," Irving says, "every novel of mine is predestined." That is a frail, human way of understanding how God designs our life's trajectory before we are born: this set of parents, this birthplace, this school, these friends, these talents and appearance, these disasters and challenges—all contribute to our life work and end. The human genius plotting the novel gives us a glimpse of how beautifully intricate the story lines of our lives must be, weaving both light and dark together.

We may never know how all the details mesh; it may be easier to see in fiction. The novel can also show us how a person fulfills his or her high calling, which may be murkier in daily life. Literature points us in the right direction. If we locate holiness outside ourselves, there is a danger of idolatry. But if we know that through Jesus' incarnation, death, and resurrection, we share his divinity, then our lives are finely calibrated, splendidly enhanced works of art: symphonies and stories.

PAUSE TO REFLECT

- Look at the life of someone you love (friend, spouse, child) as a work of art. Where do you see the genius of God and humans co-operating?

- Was it easier to see the creative trajectory of grace here, or when you trace it through your own life?

- How does your faith help you see the connection between divine story and human story?

step 7

Elegant Detail

For it was you who formed my inward parts;
*   you knit me together in my mother's womb.*
I praise you, for I am fearfully and wonderfully made....
*   My frame was not hidden from you,*
when I was being made in secret,
*   intricately woven in the depths of the earth.* PSALM 139:13–15

We often admire the craftsmanship of the cosmos: the marvels of solar system, ocean tides, rainforests, and mountains.

Yet, how often do we see the same elegance within our lives? Consider the chances of meeting your spouse or best friend—one in a million? How did you happen to connect when there were 900 other kids in that high school or 567 kids at camp that week?

The precise fit between a person and a home, a school, a region of the country, or a life work can't be random; it must be carefully choreographed. Even details of timing are orchestrated: we missed the car crash by minutes, or got the last seat on a flight, arriving home before a loved one died. If we were *in* the car crash or missed the flight, faith still attributes the plan to God. We believe that if we are wondrously made in God's image and redeemed by Christ, even the disasters are part of the plan. Surely if we tried to control all the details, making them Pollyanna-perfect, we would not leave room for the mystery of God which works through dark as well as light.

Navajo weaving and Vincent van Gogh

Two examples from the arts point to the vital role imperfections and disappointments can play. The first comes from Navajo weaving. Somewhere in every blanket a thin line, clearly not part of the pattern, reaches to the edge. This is the spirit path by which the weaver travels out of the rug so she may create more. (How closely connected the art and spirituality are here!) Other traditions include a deliberate flaw because only God can create perfection.

The second comes from the life of artist Vincent van Gogh. His painting "Starry Night" sprays light across the canvas, yet would not be so brilliant were it not for its dark background. Surely the artist poured his personal struggle into the work. Denied his heart's desire to become a minister, and desperate for money, he tried painting.

He writes of that turning point in almost religious terms: "in spite of everything I shall rise again; I will take up my pencil, which I have forsaken in my great discouragement, and I will go on with my drawing; and from that moment everything seemed transformed for me." Because of his rejection by the seminary, humanity has been enriched by his sunflowers and cypresses, enlightened by the stars strewn across his night.

So too as God creates our lives, we can marvel at details as small as chips in a mosaic, coming together to create the "big picture." Just as a novelist will introduce a detail in chapter 3 that doesn't prove important until chapter 12, so too God carefully plants seeds in childhood that may materialize in adulthood. We all know stories of the disappointment that led to miraculous growth, the split-second timing that speaks of elegant divine design.

A talent we may have overlooked for years suddenly emerges when a person or situation encourages it. A person who seems trapped in stagnancy suddenly blossoms. We discover the job that brings out the best in us or a setting where we are at home. At such times, we are amazed by the combination of forces working together that could come only from the master artist's hand.

STEPPING STONES

Accepting the 1995 Nobel Prize for Literature, the Irish poet Seamus Heaney traced his writing career back to voices he overheard on the radio as a child. These "portals in time" coaxed him to journey into the wideness of the world. His metaphor for how details came together resonates with one in this book: "a journey where each point of arrival turned out to be a stepping stone, rather than a destination."

I've had marvelous opportunities to give talks through some bizarre chains of events: someone reads my book; another speaker gets sick and I'm asked to substitute. A chance conversation over a meal leads to a long friendship. An apparently random seating arrangement places us next to the person who becomes our spouse. Is it coincidence or is it grace? Only God knows the answer.

A cartoon shows a sophisticated wife telling friends about her husband, "Arthur knows everything about theater, except how to enjoy it." As with theater, the joy of a Beethoven symphony is listening to it, not reading about it, studying it, or discussing it. So too with life—the meaning comes in living it, relishing details we may not even see or think important.

PAUSE TO REFLECT

- Fear of failure or the reality of frustration stunt many peoples' growth as artists and as human beings. They simply quit trying. How do the examples from the Navajo rugs and van Gogh's life speak to these blocks?

PRAYER

Creator God,
help me see your hand at work
in the details of my life.
Lead me to trust that even the
flaws and disappointments
can bring blessing.
I yearn for meaning in my life;
show me how even the tiniest bits
make the great mosaic.

TAKE A STEP FORWARD

Spend one day observing how details come together for you. Spend a week looking for a pattern: what is God trying to say through the small bits of your experience? How might they form a larger mosaic?

YOUR THOUGHTS

_____

_____

_____

_____

_____

_____

_____

Another Look at Faith

How do you define "faith"? How do you define "artful living"?

If you start this journey with the image of God as artist, then you can explore a way to create a life that is an artwork. You'll discover that you work in cahoots with God. You're collaborating, not trying to please some distant deity whom you can never fully satisfy. Furthermore, you have splendid role models: surely Jesus lived an artful life. Anyone who has studied John's gospel, its grand design and intricate detail, knows it is a consummate work of art.

We are born into an even larger, richer heritage of art. When people's longing for God bursts beyond words, they fly on what Michael Farrell calls "wings of 'what if?'" From the first symbols scratched on the walls of the catacombs to Gregorian chant or the rose window of Chartres, Christian art has always been a pillar of our belief system.

Those who have collaborated on a project with a business partner or a spouse know the joy and camaraderie which can emerge from shared interests and efforts. They may also know the pitfalls of partnership. But God-as-partner is even more perfect, working with us, never against, never failing us but always bringing us to the best we can be. "I am confident of this, that the one who began a good work among you will bring it to completion," we read in Philippians 1:6.

That concept adds dimensions to the life of faith that we may not have considered and underscores the uniqueness of each life. No one compares the Greek temple with the Gothic cathedral. Each has its own style and beauty.

GOD HAS A DREAM FOR YOU

So too, theologians tell us, each person has an inner truth which conforms to a creative idea in the mind of God. As St. Ignatius said, "God has a dream for you." We can spend much of our lives trying to discover this ideal, then trying to achieve whatever God dreamed for us. We can speak of a perfect rose as having everything that flower should. So the saints achieve God's ideal for human beings. So we too can learn to stand in our own truth, the best place in the world for us, the only place to be.

Ancient philosophers identified the main values of human life as truth, goodness, and beauty. While the three are interrelated, religious education in the past has focused on the first two. This book turns to the last one, beauty, as a door to the sacred and an opening to deeper, fuller human experience.

In *Six Great Ideas*, Mortimer Adler writes:

The enjoyment of beauty is not confined to the lives of those who have the habit of visiting museums, attending concerts or ballets, going to the theater, or reading poetry. It occurs also in the lives of those who are baseball, basketball, or football fans, those who go to bullfights, those who watch tennis matches, and so on.

The sports spectator who, beholding an extraordinary play or action, cries out, "wow, that's beautiful," is experiencing the same enjoyment or disinterested pleasure that is experienced by the auditor of an extraordinary performance of a Beethoven quartet.... (New York: Macmillan, 1981, 129)

Environmentalists have given us a new sense of nature's elegant beauty, its divine design. Just as we cherish the setting for human life in plains, mountains, or coastal areas, so too we can see the beauty of lives lived like jewels within these environments.

The artful life balances activity and rest. Sometimes we work hard, like a writer revising for the umpteenth time or like any of us who work to forge healthy human relationships.

But sometimes we rest, as God did on the seventh day. Some call this contemplation—when we can fully enjoy "all that God has done." It is the human activity that most closely parallels that of souls in heaven, enjoying the beatific vision. It lifts us out of ourselves and the concerns which can become petty and all-consuming. Sometimes when we relax, we see how much is grace, how much is simply given, how we could trust more.

Another dimension of faith is its reach into the unseen, its trust in things which can't be scientifically proven. Without imagination, it would be impossible to think who God might be or what heaven is like. These elements contribute to an understanding of what faith is, especially in its relationship to art. What faith is not, then, includes:

- creedal statements,
- following rules,
- an independent, lonely pursuit,
- a defense of God, morality, or church,
- easy answers to human tragedies, or
- facile solutions to complex problems.

What is faith? It's belonging to a community that shares the vision of Jesus, working to make this world more beautiful and just.

Pause to reflect

- Now that you have read this chapter, how would you answer the two questions that begin it?
- Look back over your baby pictures and think on all you have learned, achieved, and become since they were taken. Are you inspired to say, "You've come a long way, baby!" or "Good job, God!"? (Maybe both would be correct.) Beyond mastering complex skills like walking, talking, reading, driving, etc., what other tools have you learned? In what do you take most pride? In what does God delight?

Your thoughts

_____

_____

_____

_____

_____

_____

_____

_____

_____

_____

Another Look at Ourselves

Busy. How often do you hear people use that word, or use it yourself? It's become so common, we compare notes to see who's *more* busy.

And yet, if you look at what fills our days to overflowing, it's often drudgery. Home maintenance alone is a full-time job. If you have children, that means shlepping to school, the orthodontist, soccer—you know the drill. If you work, it consumes a huge number of hours, many of them spent on trivia.

Yet something resists. Aren't we more than workhorses? Don't we want more out of life? Besieged by deadlines and demands for more of our time, talent, and energy, we long for peace. We want to recapture that part of ourselves which is divine.

The question struck me as I drove to work one Monday, after a weekend filled with chores. Because it was early summer, that meant plant tomatoes, buy flowers, pay bills, answer e-mail, shop for groceries, and do laundry. Where had the weekend gone? Why, with so many jobs done, did it seem so empty?

Then, a favorite song played on the radio. It reminded me of someone I love and I sang along. For a few minutes in the car, I was carried beyond the little concerns to a better, deeper me. I could've been waltzing beneath the stars or watching the waves roll onto the beach. I was more than the weekend "to do" list.

My experience with music wasn't unusual. An Alzheimer's patient who can remember little else can still, with help from a CD, belt out the gospel songs of his Baptist boyhood. Thousands of North American women listen to the Italian love songs of Andrea Bocelli, not understanding a word, but imagining him singing to them. A cancer patient, making long drives to chemotherapy treatments, plays the same songs over and over.

When I was frightened and thought I couldn't make one more trip, I played those songs to get me there. Afterward, when I was tired and afraid I couldn't make the drive home, I played them again. My spirits never failed to recover, and the miles just flew by. In the midst of the darkest time of my life, that voice made me feel grateful to be alive.

There's a song for everyone, one incalculable mix of melody and magic that so neatly wraps the heart that we are lifted out of the here and now. And something in us is healed. (Nancy Burke, in "Meditations for Health," quoted by Frederic and Mary Ann Brussat, in *Spiritual Literacy*, New York: Simon & Schuster, 1996, 303)

So too a skillful movie leaves us feeling that the world is a good place, that evil will be beaten, and that the couple who obviously belong together will live happily after. It gives us the positive perspective which Paul's letter to the Philippians encouraged:

Finally, beloved, whatever is true, whatever is honorable, whatever is just, whatever is pure, whatever is pleasing, whatever is commendable, if there is any excellence and if there is anything worthy of praise, think about these things. (4:8)

Isn't this lifting our sights the role of art and of faith as well? Both make us better, larger people. Two stories describe a lifting-up-and-beyond like my experience in the car. The first describes art; the second, faith.

In *What Is the Point of Being a Christian?* (New York: Continuum, 2005), Timothy Radcliffe, OP, describes a visit to a part of Cairo that tourists never see, where the rubbish pickers live. It reeks of dirt and poverty. The peoples' daily activity is retrieving and sorting garbage to see what can be salvaged. But on the cliffs behind the city, a Polish artist has painted Christ's glorious resurrection, ascension, and second coming. The art reminds the people that they are also citizens of another, lovelier realm.

So too the children of ancient Greece might walk through squalid streets, but looking up, they would see the Parthenon, glistening white beneath a cobalt sky. Disease and early death plagued Europeans of the middle ages, but they could view the spire of Salisbury Cathedral. Exhausted after a day of back-breaking work, they could rejoice in the stained glass windows of Notre Dame. By showing us beauty, art calls us to our best selves, made for a kingdom where tears are wiped away and sorrows end.

This is exactly what Jesus did in his Sermon on the Mount. In her book *Embracing Our Blessings: Faces of the Beatitudes*, Kathleen Chesto explains that the beatitudes aren't simply another list of impossible tasks. The Jews used blessings to acknowledge the good things God had made for them. They knew they were surrounded by countless sparks of the holy. Their blessings didn't make a thing holy, but recognized the holiness already present.

When Jesus looked out at the crowd, he saw beyond the poverty and oppression that were surely present. He saw in their eyes the beginning of God's reign and the future promise of great things to come. Chesto points out that Jesus would've walked among the people as he spoke, touching them, inviting them to recognize their gifts and to see themselves as their creator saw them: wildly, abundantly blessed.

That may not have been how they saw themselves. That may not be how we see ourselves. We may still blame ourselves for serious mistakes. We wonder if we're on the right track or if we will ever get there. We may still not understand how unexpected shifts have added new colors to our canvas. But that is how God saw them. That is how God sees us.

PAUSE TO REFLECT

- We can believe that God creates great things. But can we believe that we are great because God is constantly creating us? Why or why not?
- Recall a time when you were lifted beyond your ordinary routine. What brought you to a better place? Was it a snatch of music, a homily, a Bible passage, a statue, beauty of nature, or work of art? Describe your experience.
- Imagine God speaking to you as one of the most stunning creatures ever made. What does God say in praise? How do you respond to God's compliment?

YOUR THOUGHTS

_____

_____

_____

_____

_____

step 10

Beauty Beyond Beauty, Endless Sea

The title of this tenth step is taken from Catherine of Siena's name for God. Source and summit of all beauty, God gives us beauty in forms we can hear, taste, see, smell, and touch as a window to God's self.

What distinguishes the artful life from one which is kind or compassionate? It may be an emphasis on beauty. Beauty has been one of the traditional proofs for God's existence. Jesuit poet Gerard Manley Hopkins called God "beauty's self and beauty's giver."

Beauty speaks as clearly to our century as to earlier ones. A 2006 statement from the Pontifical Council for Culture said, "[Beauty] has recently [reaffirmed] itself as a path to reach God, supreme beauty, and to transmit something of God's life to humankind." Timothy Radcliffe, former master general of the Dominicans, addressed the needs of this generation at Westminster Cathedral in May 2005:

> As Christians, we share our hope, for each person and for humanity. We really are on our way to happiness. And one way that we express that hope is through beauty....

Modern Europeans are resistant to church teaching. Dogma is a bad word! But beauty has its own authority, an authority to which every human being responds, and an authority that in no way threatens. We need to find ways of disclosing God's beauty to our contemporaries. We must give people a glimpse of Christ's beauty, for as Augustine said:

He is beautiful in Heaven, beautiful on earth…
beautiful in his miracles;
beautiful under the scourge
beautiful when inviting to life;
beautiful also when not regarding death
beautiful in laying down his life;
beautiful in taking it up again;
beautiful on the cross;
beautiful in the sepulcher;
beautiful in heaven…

Every great revival of Christianity has gone with some new exploration of beauty….Surely this Cathedral is an attempt to give us a glimpse of Paradise, sustaining us in the belief that the journey is going somewhere, and that one day we shall arrive.

Where else but in a gracious creator could we find the origin of spring? Its surge of new growth, its glossy greens that frame floating dogwood, lilac, redbud, and apple blossom: these could only have been created by an artist whose skills transcend the human. Who else but God could create a snow-covered meadow or mountain, symbols of "the peace that surpasses understanding"? The ocean speaks to us of infinity. Only an infinite God could have formed its endless depths, powerful waves, and shadings of color.

When we think of the staggering variety of creation—the colors, textures, scents, shapes, and sounds that God lavishly poured into this world—there is surely enough beauty for a lifetime. The church has always honored beauty as a door to the sacred. Poet Mary Oliver says "poetry...lifts the latch and gives a glimpse into a greater paradise" (*A Poetry Handbook*, San Diego: Harcourt, 1994, 9).

If the beauty of God's creation points to God's existence, surely the beauty formed and shaped by human hands glorifies God too.

If there is no point in living, if it is indeed the absurd and futile exercise some proclaim, then why do authors painstakingly revise the novel or musicians endlessly rehearse the symphony? Made in the image of God, human efforts to create beauty also prove God's existence and creative character. Those who create often find that in their work they find their greatest accord with God: both they and God delight in a laborious process which often surprises with unexpected grace.

A book I read to my children when they were small, *Miss Rumphius*, illustrated by Barbara Cooney, tells of the human creation of beauty. In it a little girl is told to make the world more beautiful. When she grows up, she sows flower seeds, and indeed, beautifies her part of the planet.

PAUSE TO REFLECT

- Where in your ordinary day do you encounter beauty?
- What are your favorite beautiful places? Imagine yourself in one of them. What do you hear? see? taste? touch? smell?

PRAYER

O Beauty ever ancient, ever new, late have I loved you!...You called, you shouted, and you broke through my deafness. You flashed, you shone, and you dispelled my blindness. You breathed your fragrance on me; I drew in breath and now I pant for you. I have tasted you, now I hunger and thirst for more. You touched me, and I burned for your peace.

—St. Augustine

RELEVANT QUOTES

I cannot believe that the inscrutable universe turns on an axis of suffering; surely the strange beauty of the world must somewhere rest on pure joy. —LOUISE BOGAN

Beauty is the visible form of the good....A flowering of beauty has drawn its sap precisely from the mystery of the Incarnation....This world in which we live needs beauty in order not to sink into despair. Beauty, like truth, brings joy to the human heart. —JOHN PAUL II, "LETTER TO ARTISTS"

Beauty will save the world.
—FYODOR DOSTOEVSKY, *The Idiot*

YOUR THOUGHTS

_____

_____

_____

_____

_____

_____

_____

_____

_____

_____

Crafting a Life

Let your light shine before others, so that they may see your good works and give glory to your Father in heaven. MATTHEW 5:16

Some days we can barely survive under a mountain of stuff to do. We consider ourselves lucky if we accomplished one thing: today I took a shower. We remember only what we didn't do or did badly. On such days, the last thing we can think about is crafting life artistically. Just getting through is a major achievement.

Yet art and religion spring from the same root: the desire to overcome our littleness. Faith calls us to more than survival. It invites us to bring all our gifts to our tasks and honor God in doing them. Then in faith, we rest, knowing that even if we didn't finish the "to do" list, we are still God's beloved.

Art helps close the gap between faith and reality. Maybe reality at the moment looks like pond scum. But art lifts us up to the beauty we were born for. Art reminds us that we belong to God and nothing less will ever fulfill us. The combination of art and faith is a unique way of seeing beyond the current reality, knowing that it isn't everything.

In both the arts and faith, the human spirit triumphs over every machine that tries to grind us down to less than we are: corporate greed, environmental exploitation, sexism, racism, ageism, or idiotic government policies. "I am more than a cog in your machine," says the artist or faith-filled person. "I create my art and my life with a unique voice that can't be bent to institutional uses or sold for profit. However I make the statement 'Here I am,' it's a banner of freedom hung beyond anyone's control."

My father was still crafting a faithful life at the age of ninety-three in the retirement center where he lived. One day, however, crisis struck. The elevator broke and those who lived on the second floor were stranded without access to activities on the first floor. The staff worked hard to alleviate the problem, but the elevator repair was complex and time-consuming.

The elderly residents didn't like any changes in their routines. The chorus of grumbling reached its peak at a "town meeting" where they complained loudly about incompetence. Then my father spoke. "The staff here has been so kind during this crisis, trying so hard to minimize it," he said gently. "I think we should give them a standing ovation." Then he looked around at all the walkers and wheelchairs. "I mean that figuratively," he added wryly. "Not literally."

Everyone broke into laughter; the mood in the room shifted from crotchety to appreciative. My father was living artfully.

In some way, the story holds the theme of all great art and religion: the constant movement of our days between light and dark, peaks and pits, kindness and meanness, joy and sorrow, life and death. Sometimes we go through all that in a week, sometimes in an hour.

RELEVANT QUOTES

All the arts we practice are apprenticeship. The big art is our life.
—M.C. RICHARDS

The main thing, of course, always is the fact that there is only one of you in the world, just one, and if that is not fulfilled then something has been lost. —MARTHA GRAHAM

You say grace before meals. All right. But I say grace before the concert and the opera, and grace before the play and pantomime, and grace before I open a book, and grace before sketching, painting, and swimming, fencing, boxing, walking, playing, dancing, and grace before I dip the pen in ink.

—G.K. CHESTERTON

Creativity is...seeing something that doesn't exist already. You need to find out how you can bring it into being and that way be a playmate with God. —MICHELE SHEA

PAUSE TO REFLECT

- Name people you know who have crafted artful lives. Now focus on one who might be a model for you.

- How might it make your daily routine different to think of your life as art?

STOP FOR A MOMENT

Spend a little time here looking back over the first part of this book. Which chapters touched you most profoundly? Which challenged you? Share with someone or reflect alone on the insights you are gaining as a result of these stepping stones to the artful life.

The Art of the Ordinary

I am not the queen of domesticity. But I try to bake treats for friends having a rough time. I do it because it has meant so much to me when they have brought goodies, warm and fragrant, during crises in my own life. One day, delivering a coffee cake to a friend whose husband had just undergone excruciating cancer surgery, I thought, how frail these offerings we place on the altar of suffering. They are such small appeasements.

Posed against our certain mortality: a salad.

Held up to the principalities and powers of darkness: a casserole.

Flaunting the terrible tragedies and unredeemed pain: muffins.

It is all we can do, but it is everything. It may seem fragile, but it must be done. If we ignore these little gestures, we do not follow the Holy One who became incarnate, dwelling in a frail human tent. This great God of ours is intimate, too, spanning the universe, yet entering small and simple rooms.

In her book *The Quotidian Mysteries*, Kathleen Norris writes of first seeing a Catholic Mass. What strikes her most is the "clerical clean-up." She whispers to friends, "He's doing the dishes!" "I found it enormously comforting to see the priest as a kind of daft housewife, overdressed for the kitchen...puttering about the altar, washing up after having served so great a meal to so many people."

She goes on to muse that if our holiest activity ends with something so menial, then the reverse might also be true. In the dailiness lies our salvation. Indeed, one way we gauge mental illness is that those who suffer from it can't muster the energy for the ordinary chores: getting out of bed, washing hair or clothes, fixing a meal, bathing. We are grounded by cooking, cleaning, or whatever task we do even though we may resent its repetition or mindlessness.

One reason we haven't recognized the worth of daily work is that for centuries most of it was women's work, while men did the "important jobs." This attitude carries over into the church, where even today, males make the decisions while women make the coffee.

We're lucky to live during a shift away from huge heroism to the holiness in small things. A Zen saying captures this change:

Before enlightenment: chopping wood, carrying water.
After enlightenment: chopping wood, carrying water.

The work is the same, yet a great shift occurs when we realize: if we must do it anyway, why not do it with an inner awareness that makes it artful? When we're muttering to ourselves, "If I could just get outta this kitchen, this cubicle, this school!" we may miss the shining of our God-likeness in these ordinary settings. The eye of faith transforms the ordinary, shown in the old example of one man thinking he's simply laying brick; another bricklayer proudly contributes to the majesty of Canterbury cathedral.

Christian tradition has always connected the earthy to the spiritual. The Benedictines reverence the tools for garden and kitchen as much as the altar vessels.

POEM

THE CANA COUPLE REMINISCE

That was only the beginning:
   acned and awkward we were then,
   embarrassed enough without the wine incident,
   indebted to Mary's son for the flow of joy.

Ever since it has been miracle:
   touching the shoreline of the other in our sleep,
   waking warm beneath our roof,
   hoeing the wheat shoots in our fields.

Even the threats brought blessing:
   brooding death intensified our life,
   illness taught nurture of cherished child,
   the needy repaid us with Cana's own poor gold.

Our union was not singular; we fought
   and sulked, sickened like the other folks.
But in every glass of common water,
   we tasted hints of garnet-gold.

RELEVANT QUOTES

I now require this of all pictures, that they domesticate me, not that they dazzle me.　　　—RALPH WALDO EMERSON

With the happiness held in one inch-square heart you can fill the whole space between heaven and earth.
　　　—GENSEI, SEVENTEENTH-CENTURY BUDDHIST MONK

PAUSE TO REFLECT

- Do you, like most of us, tend to admire powerful "movers and shakers" more than the maids who clean their rooms or the cooks who fix their meals? Given that the powers-that-be cause disastrous wars, global greed, and needless human suffering, why do most of us still have this bias in their favor?

- If we have a day when something disastrous happens, we long for the ordinary. Why does it take such a sharp contrast to help us appreciate our routines?

PRAYER

O Father, light up the small duties of this day's life:
  may they shine with the beauty of your countenance.
May we believe that glory can dwell
  in the commonest task of every day.

—ST. AUGUSTINE

ACTION SUGGESTION

Name one everyday activity you don't mind—doing laundry, cooking, washing the car, cleaning, taking out trash. This week, focus on reverently making this job an art. Try to transform the ordinary task into building God's reign on earth. How does this deliberate frame of mind affect the way you work?

YOUR THOUGHTS

_____

_____

_____

_____

_____

_____

The Diva of the Daily

I thank you, Father, Lord of heaven and earth, because you have hidden these things from the wise and the intelligent and have revealed them to infants. LUKE 10:21

The model for divas of the daily is Jesus who said, "the reign of God is within you." In touch with markets, smells, disease, and boredom, he knew the earthy as well as the divine. He spoke with a new authority based on direct experience. He believed that God dwells within.

Jesus rarely engaged in abstract philosophy. He always preferred the fish and the boat, the lamp on the basket, the touch on the forehead. Jesus knew the art of the ordinary when he told a story of a woman sweeping her house or kneading her dough. No lightning bolts; no victorious armies; no avalanches. But women doing ordinary jobs teach spiritual truths. They tell of a God who pursues the lost human with the vigor she hunts her lost coin. They show us the face of the unknown God who kneads dough with spirit and grace.

Jesus' earthy attitude carries over into the Eucharistic Prayer:

Through him you give us all these gifts.
You fill them with life and goodness.
You bless them and make them holy.

We might each complete a specific list of "all these gifts" to establish clearly where we find God. Then, like the poet Billy Collins, we could sing "a homemade canticle of thanks."

Different characters in Scripture have a harder time following Jesus' artful wedding of daily with divine. The Samaritan woman can't get beyond the need for water from the well (John 4:1–42). When Jesus offers her living water, she reminds him bluntly, "You have no bucket, and the well is deep." Finally, he convinces her with a promise of "water gushing up to eternal life."

Peter also fails to see the connections. He is shocked that something as dusty as foot washing could be God's work (John 13:5–12). He protests, "You will never wash my feet." But Jesus makes it the condition of friendship with him. Leadership in his reign never consists of "lording it over" another. His leaders do the work of women and slaves.

The story of Elisha the prophet in the Old Testament has a similar respect for daily work. He so appreciated the lamp, the bed, the table and chair kindly provided by the Shunammite woman that he promised her her heart's desire: "At this season, in due time, you shall embrace a son" (2 Kings 4:16).

POEM

DUSTING ST. FRANCIS

Only the soft, orange-scented cloth will do
   the pearled film of oil on wooden
   shoulders crafted from a rough log,
   dusted reverently—do not disturb curly
   bark or perching birds. The statue echoes
   Santa Fe where its lines were carved.

His niche on a bookshelf
   softened by candlelight
   which plays across the face so

sometimes his sad eyes grieve the world
and sometimes his wry grin asks like Puck,
"In the end, what loss is not restored?"

He tickles my curmudgeon self, nudging me
to remember honeysuckle and warm adobe
rounded against crystalline skies of
New Mexico, or maybe Assisi with Clare.
Francis sturdy as a branch, grace our
wintry days with tight buds of joy.

PRAYER

Thank you, God, for
the miracle of the ordinary,
the blessings of small things.
Help us weave the details of our days
into a canticle of praise.

SCRIPTURE

"While they were eating, Jesus took a loaf of bread, and after blessing it he broke it, and gave it to the disciples and said, 'take, eat; this is my body'" (Matthew 26:26). Notice that Jesus' most characteristic action, by which we remember him today, occurs during a meal, with all the commotion, noise, clanking of silver and spilling of milk that implies. He isn't removed from the chaos in which most of us live our lives.

Note that he didn't take lobster, steak, or a rare tropical fruit, but an ordinary food which most people throughout the world eat daily, in some form. What other evidence do you find in the gospel that he was truly in touch with the gritty everyday that constitutes most peoples' lives?

ACTION SUGGESTION

Create your own "homemade canticle of thanks." What small, daily miracles would you include?

YOUR THOUGHTS

_____

_____

_____

_____

_____

_____

_____

_____

_____

_____

_____

_____

_____

_____

step 14

The Art of Transformation

Picture this scene. An ugly grey cement factory in western Canada adjoins a limestone quarry beneath leaden skies. After mining all the limestone for cement, only a pit remains. Many people would say "yuck," or move to a sunnier climate. Jennie and Robert Butchart have a different vision.

Starting with one rose bush and a packet of sweet pea seed, they plant a garden which, one hundred years later, is the world famous Butchart Gardens, visited by over a million people a year. The quarry becomes a sunken garden beside a lake where the fountain spouts jets in a graceful ballet. Rhododendrons the colors of fiestas splash British Columbia with Key West sunsets. A cascade of apricot like a Guatemalan market provides the backdrop for a Blue Tibetan poppy. A cozy cove becomes the site for picnics, boating, and swimming. In the 1920s, when over 50,000 people visited annually, they named their estate Benvenuto, the Italian word for "welcome."

If that sounds too easy, the archives hold pictures of horse-drawn carts lugging loads of topsoil to the quarry in 1912. The flannel skies which provide ample watering for the plants can also dispense a depressing overload of rain. And yet, driven by their vision, they pushed on to "create anew."

Jennie and Robert Butchart lived with the same tough realities we all face. Yet their partnership flourished. She gave up a scholarship to study art in Paris when she married him. He passed all credit for their achievements to her. He got caught up in the garden project too, training the trout in one pond to surface when he clapped. Their grandson Ian Ross who inherited the gardens, called them his grandmother's diamond, for which his grandfather provided the setting.

Seeing through it all

Anyone else might see a drug addict or alcoholic, feel pity, and wonder why they ruined their life. Killian Noe sees beneath the crusty surface to God's beloved child. She co-founded the Samaritan Inns in the District of Columbia and the Recovery Café in Seattle to help those trapped in addictions. For the many who have been abused, the radical news of unconditional love is translated into fresh flowers, clean bathrooms, a place where everybody knows your name—circles of support and accountability.

Killian writes,

> They not only hear this message of how loved they are, they see it in the beauty of the space into which they have been welcomed, they taste it in the delicious and nutritious food they are served, they feel it as they crawl between the clean sheets of their sturdy beds each night and sleep without fear of being assaulted. (*Finding Our Way Home: Addictions and Divine Love*, Scottsdale, PA: Herald Press, 2003, 13)

Firmly believing that God's dream is to pour out love onto every human being, Killian, her staff, and those who support them with prayer and money cooperate with God's work in a difficult arena.

They teach everyone the practice of centering prayer, and follow up with practical steps like money management plans.

They compare their work to the prophet Elisha's, who prayed, then stretched his own body across the body of a dead child. He breathed his own breath into the boy, and restored his life. The situations of homeless addicts are so serious that they demand all the energy and resources the helper has.

And amazing transformations have resulted. A prostitute who would pass out every night in a different crack house becomes a responsible mother, completes a college degree, and works full-time as a hospital nurse. A girl who watched her mother kill her abusive father celebrates two years free from heroin. A gang member gives up his gun. While no treatment is fool-proof, the treatment Killian and others like her have developed gives many people a giant step toward transformation.

Such "artists of transformation" follow Jesus who had a remarkable knack for it. He once left a synagogue where everyone was filled with rage, wanting to hurl him off a cliff. Luke records: "But he passed peacefully through the midst of them and went on his way" (4:30).

A commitment to Alcoholics Anonymous, a diet, or an exercise program can transform one who's faithful to it. So too, following Christ through the doors of trust eventually transforms his disciple. God's shaping of a life has been compared to a potter's molding clay. We may fuss and strain as we are bent and stretched to God's design, but eventually we become God's artwork.

SCRIPTURE

If any one is in Christ, there is a new creation.
— 2 CORINTHIANS 5:17

God's mercies never come to an end; they are new every morning.
— LAMENTATIONS 3:22–23

RELEVANT QUOTES

I merely took the energy it takes to pout and wrote some blues.
—DUKE ELLINGTON

No pessimist ever discovered the secret of the stars or sailed an uncharted land, or opened a new doorway for the human spirit.
—HELEN KELLER

PAUSE TO REFLECT

Only in looking back over a period of time do we see how far we've come. Name one way you have been transformed

—in the last year

—in the last five years

—in the last ten years.

YOUR THOUGHTS

———————————————————————

———————————————————————

———————————————————————

———————————————————————

———————————————————————

———————————————————————

———————————————————————

———————————————————————

The Art of Parenting

When Israel was a child, I loved him,
and out of Egypt I called my son.
The more I called them,
the more they went from me....
Yet it was I who taught Ephraim to walk,
I took them up in my arms;
but they did not know that I healed them.
I led them with cords of human kindness,
with bands of love.
I was to them like those
who lift infants to their cheeks.'
I bent down to them and fed them.
How can I give you up, Ephraim?
How can I hand you over, O Israel? HOSEA 11:1–4, 8

She approaches mysteriously in the twilight from the underbrush, tawny, graceful and pure. She looks at me with such innocence, I begin to understand the expression "doe-eyed."

Just behind Mama Deer is a small, brown, speckled fawn who puts into motion Gerard Manley Hopkins's line, "Glory be to God for dappled things." I pause and describe the lovely creatures to my son who's on the cell phone, not wanting him to miss it. He's thirty-three now, but I probably use the same tone I did when he was five. If something awesome appeared, I'd whisper, "Look!"

Later I see the link between the two pairs of mother and child, animal and human. That archetype nestles deep in our faith with many images of Madonna and Christ child.

Jesus grew up hearing his mother's Magnificat, which shaped his identification with the hungry, poor, and grieving. Over his watery baptism floated the father's words, "This is my beloved child; in you I take delight." In the art of parenting, as in any other art, the first, best modeling is God's.

Many of us are bewildered about parenting young adults, but Mary provides a role model here. Her communication to Jesus at Cana is direct and succinct: "They have no wine." Then she waits—as parents must often do.

We wait for the first nine months, through croup and flu and sleepless nights, through the silences of adolescence, through prom night when the door clicks shut at 4 AM, through college or the military, dating and engagements, then back to the nine-month wait for grandchildren. At both Cana and Calvary, Mary shows us how to stand back when every instinct shouts, "Rush in! Protect!"

Some may see parenting as the hardest work they've ever done, which is true. But it's also more: it's an art. Knowing when to laugh or cry, punish or relent, encourage or discourage, pick the battle or wave the white flag ultimately comes down to the rhythm of experience and a firm connection with the divine parent.

The best parents, like artists, learn early on how to play with their children, recovering their own playfulness. Sometimes it just means slowing down to say, "Look!" That cry of wonder alerts our offspring not only to deer, but to all the wonders God places in our world. Many parents start out uptight, gradually learning to relax and enjoy—an art often not perfected until grandparenthood.

Brian Doyle explains parenting well: "I am rich in children, but they are driving me stark raving muttering insane." He then shifts, as we all do, to the saner stance:

I am a man wealthy beyond words in the only coin that matters, love, harried though it may be.

There are many shapes and forms of love, all of them slippery and nutritious, but to love and be loved by children is maybe the most complex and mysterious of all. In a real sense it is the bedrock of human persistence and culture, the sort of broad unconscious love we must rise to, or die choking in the world we have irredeemably fouled.

The parent suspects that the sloppy depth of love for a child surpasses anything else we do in this life. As Doyle concludes, "I try to keep this in mind even when the shrill shrieking in my house causes me to use bad words and hide in the basement" (*Leaping*, Chicago: Loyola Press, 2003, 180–81).

Relevant quote

Here is someone I would die for....Were you amazed to find yourself thinking this when you held your first child in your arms? Motherhood can bring out the best in us, often much to our own surprise. We find we are capable of sacrifices we couldn't contemplate before. We now have another bond with Jesus, who also gave his life for people he loved beyond measure.

—Catherine O'Connell-Cahill

Pause to reflect

- If you have children or grandchildren, would you agree that parenting is an art? Why or why not?
- When have you risen to artistic heights as a parent or nurturer? What were the circumstances and what did you do that you're proud of?

The Art of Writing

As a child I was a Nancy Drew mystery addict and a klutz at sports. My favorite activity was writing stories and reading them to a captive audience of dolls. They would sit in neatly arranged small chairs and offer the same fixed smiles to everything I said, no matter how outrageous. I guess it was good preparation for someone who'd grow up to be a writer.

After two degrees in English literature and a career of teaching others to write, I finally got my turn. Some teachers pass a magic threshold, when they cannot grade one more theme about the senior prom, the horrors of the roommate, or the football victory. When I'd had it with teaching, I returned to my first love.

Audiences are often intrigued by how a career in writing takes shape, as though some mysterious angel perched on one's shoulder. I simply tell them it's the only thing I'm good at. Or enjoy so much. It connects an introvert like myself to people around the world. I believe what a priest told the poet Anne Sexton: "God is in your typewriter." (Only now he'd say "computer.")

Writing intersects with the art of faith in many ways. Perhaps the parable of the pearl captures the connection. "The kingdom of heaven is like a merchant in search of fine pearls; on finding one

57

pearl of great value, he went and sold all that he had and bought it"
(Matthew 13:45–46)

Those who've learned to read Scripture suspect the merchant is
searching for more than pearls. The pearl can symbolize our deepest longing: for God, for immortality, for the fulfilled life. It's
important that the merchant is engaged in work when he finds the
pearl. The pearl trade is his career, and we often find God not only
in our churches, but where we spend most of our time—our jobs.

MY WAY OF SPEAKING

Writing is my tool to express and probe that longing, just as van
Gogh's was a palette and brush. In trying to express this yearning, I
discover more about it—and about my bonds with other people. At
heart, we are all made for the same God. From a chair at home, I
unite with people I'll never meet. Even better, writing gives me an
immediate connection with those I *do* meet, who sound like friends
even though we've just been introduced. "I liked the story about the
pink suit!" they'll laugh. And we're on the same page. I know which
book they've read; they know me at a level beyond "hello."

But there is another longing, and that is to know who we are. I
focus on writing because I know it best and because it's my window
on all the other forms of creativity. I hope what I say about it resonates with readers' arts.

This sacred quest to find out who we are is somewhat mysterious, so I can't explain it completely. When I'm writing there's a special energy. In the act of writing I'm discovering things I didn't
know I knew.

I'm also creating beauty, a search for the precise word and the
phrases that flow together like music. I may not make the world
more just (though some friends will) or more efficient (others have
got that covered), but perhaps, a little more beautiful.

Finally, writing is an exercise in trust. Not that God will send
miraculous, fully formatted pages of wisdom just in time for the

deadline—that's magic. No, I trust the writing process. If I put in my time and energy, as I've seen over and over again, something will emerge. That something will need endless revision to make it clear, but eventually it will communicate—first to me, then to my reader. Watching a final manuscript come from an unfinished mess, seeing sloppy piles of papers transformed to a tidily bound and coherent book helps me believe "nothing is impossible with God." Writing can be slow and arduous, but sometimes it can be revelatory. It is also, like God's creation in Genesis, an attempt to bring order out of chaos.

SCRIPTURE

This is the disciple who is testifying to these things and has written them, and we know that his testimony is true. But there are also many other things that Jesus did; if every one of them were written down, I suppose that the world itself could not contain the books that would be written.   —JOHN 21:24–25

PAUSE TO REFLECT

• How do you feel about writing?

ACTION SUGGESTION

Try to free yourself of writer's block by not worrying that your writing must be perfect, error-free—or that anyone will see it. Simply write a story (or poem, ballad, script, haiku, whatever) that only you will see. Make it as long or as short as you need to. Describe a recent experience, a vacation memory, or a funny happening. Then reflect back: How was the process? As you worked, did you feel like a participant in God's larger creation?

The Art of Mending, 1

Have mercy on me, God,
  according to your steadfast love;
according to your abundant mercy
  blot out my transgressions.
Wash me thoroughly from my iniquity,
  and cleanse me from my sin.

Create in me a clean heart, O God,
  and put a new and right spirit within me.
Do not cast me away from your presence,
  and do not take your holy spirit from me.
Restore to me the joy of your salvation,
  and sustain in me a willing spirit. PSALM 51:1–2, 10–12

Remember the mending basket? In it, we stuffed the shirt that needed a button, the pants with the ripped seam, the sock with the hole. It's a sad relic by now—who has time to darn? The ripped pants get tossed in the Good Will bag and the button is lost at the bottom of the closet.

But the mending basket still works to understand the art of reconciliation. It takes an artist's critical eye to see relationships in disrepair, rips in the fabric of our lives, embarrassing failures. Our initial reaction to mending might be "ugh." Few people want to devote energy to something that sounds depressing and outmoded.

If we think of mending as restoring an original beauty, the activity has more appeal. Think of polishing a dull surface to a shiny finish. Everyone who's ever had an aching tooth filled or a painful disease cured knows the relief of returning to health. Anyone who's ever loved knows the joy of reunion after an absence, or the joy of harmony after an argument.

When we were born, God had a dream for us. We marvel at the newborn's silky wisps of hair, satiny skin, and deep eyes, forgetting that we were once that way. How can we return to being that human creature in whom God takes delight? Let's look at four different areas, in steps seventeen and eighteen, like four items pulled from the basket.

THE WORLD

> These things, these things were here and but the beholder
> Wanting.
> —GERARD MANLEY HOPKINS, "HURRAHING IN HARVEST"

How often we miss the beauty of creation: the salmon tinge of sunset, the rustle of branches in the wind, the shimmering of sun on water, the grace of a bird's flight. Many people yawn and think, "how ordinary." But the artful know how to find God's presence through the world God made. If we received a wonderful gift from a person we loved, wouldn't we explore it, treasure it, take it out often, wear it, or admire it? Yet God gives us a magnificent world each day: do we look for the Creator's hand prints there?

THE SELF

> I am fearfully and wonderfully made.   —PSALM 139:14

We've come a long way from punishing the flesh to taking better care of ourselves. There's an art in getting the rest, prayer time, exercise, and diet we deserve. Napping doesn't top most "to do" lists, but studies show many people are sleep-deprived. If we're cranky, short-tempered, and dull-witted for that reason, restoring good humor through adequate sleep might be just the ticket. Shakespeare must have been thinking of the mending basket when he described sleep as "knitting up the raveled edge of care."

Mention prayer and many people groan. They know they should; they just can't squeeze it in. But if we think of prayer as "a personal encounter with my one great Love," as St. Ignatius did, we'll find the time. Simply turning off the television can create that space for many people. We often pray better when steeped in beautiful music, surrounded by artwork or plants, gazing outside at trees or sky, smelling the fragrance of candles or flowers, reading inspirational literature. When we come to see how quiet time alone with the Lord restores serenity, trust, and balance, it becomes an invaluable part of every day.

If this body is God's temple, it's wise to keep it in good repair. A daily walk, a yoga or water aerobics class at the local Y or recreation center may add artfulness to our days. While the subject of diet is tricky, statistics indicate that most people need to forgo their fast food (sorry, but the burger and fries are a heart attack wrapped in a bun). And a few who have grown uptight and mean on their grilled fish and vegetable diet may need to savor a luscious chocolate.

While we may think we make heroic efforts, the major initiative in any mending effort is God's. The first letter of John promises the change God will work in us:

> Beloved, we are God's children now; what we will be has not yet been revealed. What we do know is this: when he is revealed, we will be like him, for we will see him as he is.
> (1 John 3:2)

To be like Christ because, seeing him, we couldn't be anything else must represent the ultimate mending. Christ transforms our poor, shoddy selves into himself and that is cause for celebration.

ACTION SUGGESTION

Today admire something God created. Tomorrow, do a kindness for yourself.

YOUR THOUGHTS

_____

_____

_____

_____

_____

_____

_____

_____

_____

_____

_____

The Art of Mending, 2

Do not judge, and you will not be judged; do not condemn, and you will not be condemned. Forgive, and you will be forgiven; give, and it will be given to you. A good measure, pressed down, shaken together, running over, will be put into your lap; for the measure you give will be the measure you get back.

How can you say to your neighbor, "Friend, let me take out the speck in your eye," when you yourself do not see the log in your own eye? You hypocrite, first take the log out of your own eye, and then you will see clearly to take the speck out of your neighbor's eye.
LUKE 6:37–38, 42

Continuing to look at areas that need repair, we turn to two other general categories or "items in the mending basket."

THE OTHER

> *The disparity between all the tenderness I've received and the amount I've given….*
>
> —GALWAY KINNELL, *The Cellist*

Homilies of the past were one-size-fits-all. The workaholics as well as the lazy were told to try harder. Aaron needed to relax and

Barbara needed to speed up, but both got the same advice. Yet anyone who's done the family mending knows the garments are individually sized. The hard challenge may be deciding what we need most and where God is directing us.

So when it comes to other people, some may need to muster their courage and walk away from a relationship that destroys integrity and undermines peace. The days when confessors encouraged women to remain in abusive marriages are fortunately past, but other unhealthy relationships may persist. Sometimes a parent is so critical of a child, that even adult offspring may need to move on to guard their mental health.

But for most of us, the mending of relationships demands more time, care, and attention lavished on those we love. How often has a harsh word scarred the child we never intended to hurt? When have we transferred our frustration at the insurance company to an innocent spouse? Have we projected stress at work onto those at home, who don't know the cause? Has failure to deal with our own angers spilled unfairly onto friends?

We may need to unravel the cozy cocoon we spin around ourselves. Whom have we neglected because "we're *so* busy"? We all know lonely people who'd love to hear from us. Could a three-minute e-mail or a five-minute phone call really be that difficult? Jesus could look at a crowd and identify the one most needing a cure. Can we find the one who longs for our attention?

GOD

In You everything is found; in You everything is forgotten.
—ST. TERESA OF AVILA

To avoid the pitfalls of the self-help manual, we must ask ourselves ultimately why we mend. If the answer isn't to deepen our relationship with God, to praise our Creator, and to love better, then we're on the wrong track. We need to remember that God seeks us passionately, desperately, responding quickly to our small efforts. Two biblical questions might guide our quest for Christ. "For whom are you looking?" Jesus asks the soldiers sent to arrest him (John 18:4). He repeats the question to Mary Magdalene, weeping at his tomb (John 20:15).

Who is Christ for us? He doesn't shift to fit our moods. But throughout a lifetime, as with any friend, our relationship changes. At different times, we may respond better to different faces of God. To broaden the question, then, we might ask ourselves which is our favorite Scripture story about Jesus, and what the choice tells us about ourselves. Which of his words do we like best?

We may want to memorize these. Then we can repeat them as quiet prayer in places where we have no Bible: the line at the grocery store or bank, the commute on the bus or train.

The second question connects directly to the mending basket.

"What do you want me to do for you?" Jesus asks blind Bartimaeus (Mark 10:46–52). It may seem obvious that the beggar wants his sight, but Jesus invites his participation in the miracle. If Jesus peered over our shoulders into the mending baskets of our lives, where would he see the need for sewing what is torn?

While we may be tempted to shrug off these questions quickly, they deserve long, slow time. This could mean an hour without TV, a day of prayer, or a weekend retreat. But what could be more important than digging deep into those answers, at a pivotal time which might shape the rest of our lives?

RELEVANT QUOTES

Love is an act of endless forgiveness, a tender look which becomes a habit.
—PETER USTINOV

Once a woman has forgiven her man, she must not reheat his sins for breakfast.
—MARLENE DIETRICH

PAUSE TO REFLECT

- What in your basket needs mending? Or, where in the four areas covered in these two steps did you squirm uncomfortably? That's a sign to look at it harder.

ACTION SUGGESTION

Is there someone from whom you feel distant, someone you need to forgive? Think about this person and what happened to cause the estrangement. Mend the rip that is between you: artfully, craftily. Then enjoy being whole again and having this person back in your life.

YOUR THOUGHTS

_____

_____

_____

_____

_____

_____

_____

_____

_____

_____

The Artful Life

We begin step nineteen with a question: What makes life artful? It may mean seeing the beautiful in the ordinary. Perhaps it is kindness toward others, gracious care for them. It may mean seasoning the bland routine, or softening it with humor. Surely there are no perfect formulas. This kind of exploration can't be placed on graphs or spread sheets. It is instead the territory of the heart, the inner life.

But stories give examples: beginning in Scripture, then mirrored in contemporary lives. One of Jesus' most artful encounters must have been his post-resurrection breakfast barbecue, recounted in John 21:1–14. How carefully he prepared the charcoal fire and arranged the fish on it. He knew how tired and hungry the disappointed fisherfolk must have been after pulling in empty nets all night. His question, wafted across the lake, "Children, you have no fish, have you?" aches with maternal tenderness. How considerately he invited the participation of his friends: "Cast the net to the right side," then "Bring some of the fish you have caught."

How he must have welcomed the blustering, soaking wet Peter, who couldn't wait for the slow oars to row him ashore, but instead plunged into the sea, eager to see the friend he had betrayed. How thoroughly Jesus understands their need: not primarily for esoteric resurrection theology, but first for relief from hunger: "Come and have breakfast." When he gives them bread and fish, he does so reverently, his scarred hands lingering on tawny loaf and silvery scales.

If we need a model of the artful life, we need look no further. But we can expand the story, with the ways other people have taken that model and incorporated it into their own lives.

BE WATCHFUL

While it may be the stuff of legend, it contains seeds of truth. Clint Eastwood planned to start an exclusive golf club near Carmel, California. He invited prominent people to a reception where he launched the idea, and explained that membership would be by invitation only. After the reception, invitations went out—but not necessarily to the most wealthy or most famous. Eastwood had carefully observed how his guests treated his staff. Those who were courteous got invited.

A GRACIOUS CUP OF TEA

George wasn't famous, but he cultivated a sense of life's daily miracles. As a painter, he was keenly aware of shapes and tones, the angle of light. But the following example may be closer to most peoples' experience. When guests visited one winter afternoon, his wife served a simple snack: tea and peanut butter cookies. Sitting at the wooden table in late afternoon sun with them was an exercise in appreciation.

George inhaled the tea's fragrance, relished its apricot taste. He was so obviously enjoying his hot "cuppa" that his wife offered refills. George's face lit up. "Why, thank you, darling!" he beamed. They had probably been married for fifty years, but she was still his dear love. He'd had serious health problems that year, but for the moment, life was beautiful: friends around a table, warmth on a cold day, tea. No British queen sipped her Earl Grey with more gratitude than George.

It would make me happy

Three weeks before my father died, my daughter and I visited him at the retirement center where he lived. The staff could not persuade him to eat vegetables before his ice cream. We sat with him at lunch, where he feebly requested ice cream. The Brunhilda who controlled the kitchen bellowed "*No*! You've got to eat your real food first!"

Once a naval officer and university professor, dad maintained his dignity. Spreading his hands in a gentle gesture, he tried again: "It would make me very happy if you could bring my guests some ice cream." He melted Brunhilda's heart. She handed us each a tiny Dixie cup of vanilla ice cream, complete with small wooden spoon.

Poem

Gesture

You rose from breakfast for
   more coffee and I knew
   I knew you'd touch my shoulder.
In the second before, I leaned
   into the sweet, cupped palm
   which brushed my skin
   like light gilding meadows
   or music cascading.

The rightness of it: the anticipating
   and the meeting in sync
   like jeweled dew nested in silky web.
The souls' two hands harmonized,
   skimming Braille text, reading
   the pebbled contours of care.

PAUSE TO REFLECT

- Five examples are given here of an artful life: Jesus, Clint Eastwood, George, the author's father, and a kind gesture. Which person would you like to have been? With which one would you like to spend an afternoon?

RELEVANT QUOTES

Art is a collaboration between God and the artist and the less the artist does the better.
—ANDRE GIDE

The position of the artist is humble. He is essentially a channel.
—PIET MONDRIAN

ACTION SUGGESTIONS

Start tomorrow to create an artful life. Waking up can mean hitting the alarm button, scratching ourselves, and dreading the day. Or we can wake with the anticipation of St. Augustine: "Each dawn is a new creation." Do one necessary chore with vigor. Beautify. Place flowers or a candle on the kitchen table. Play soothing music as you dress. Wink at that lovely critter in the mirror.

YOUR THOUGHTS

_____

_____

_____

_____

_____

The Art of Touch

I never thought I'd write about the Blessing of the Root Canal. I'd often used that dental procedure to represent intense pain. When I read a parenting book that said, "Always present your children with choices," I'd offer two: "Take out the trash or have a root canal." So when I walked into the oral surgeon's office facing the prospect myself, I felt like the ax was about to fall.

But the surgeon's touch was gentle, and understanding wimps like me, she let my daughter stay throughout the root canal. It went better than I ever dreamt it could. My last conscious thought was a foggy prayer: "Relax: God is merciful."

When I began to come out of the anesthesia, the first thing I felt was my daughter's hand on my ankle. She had sat near my feet for more than an hour and before I ever saw her, I felt her presence. "Ah," I thought woozily. "So this is why Jesus touched the people he cured." Long after eyes close and hearing dims, touch reassures. And its blessings aren't restricted to crisis situations.

When we meet someone we love we haven't seen in a long time, words don't do it. We must hug, kiss, touch. The body carries so much stress that it feels like removing a heavy burden to have it wiped away. As one masseuse told me bluntly, "Your neck is a train wreck and your back is a rock garden." During a massage, we want to stay under the care of those skillful hands, forever. It's no wonder some people weep and others fall asleep.

The warmth, the skin contact, the aroma of oil all combine to make a feast for the senses. Tension dissolves and relaxation flows down the spine. Prickly questions and pressing issues are rubbed away. What gifts a massage therapist carries in her strong hands!

Every year I make an eight-day silent retreat. After many years of the same thing happening, I know the pattern. The screaming banshees emerge to fill the vacuum. I obsess about all the worries kept on hold because I didn't have time to deal with them when they surfaced. Sitting outdoors, watching the hummingbirds battle mercilessly over the sugar water in their feeder, I think they mirror my internal state.

The hummingbird wars within me continue for several days. No amount of spiritual direction, Scripture reading, or long walks calms me down. Then it happens: the massage therapist hangs up a schedule and for me it's Holy Writ. In less than an hour, she sends the demons of stress packing.

The massage marks the turning point of the retreat. I emerge relaxed, serene, confident, faith-filled. All the other faith-building activities surely contribute to this watershed, but the therapeutic touch opens a new channel for grace. Instead of bombarding my director with my problems, I listen to her wisdom. Instead of heckling God about the hassles of the past year, I thank God for the Spirit's presence there, which I can see clearly only in hindsight. Nothing can disturb the deep inner peace. I sail forth ready to serve.

RELEVANT QUOTE

The loving touch, like music, often utters things that can't be spoken—nothing need be said, for everything is understood.
—ASHLEY MONTAGUE, *Touching*,
(NEW YORK: HARPER, 1986, 287)

POEM

MASSAGE THERAPIST

If healing has hands
they are hers. Rivers of mercy
flow down the tense neck,
the knotted muscles,
the contorted spine.

Weeks of "mind over matter"
soothed by hands that pull
like artist's brush through
rich ochre. She banishes the
demons drumming the shoulders.

Grace must be like this:
touch melting stiffness.
Miraculous, the gifts we
give each other.
Don't stop. Don't ever stop.

SCRIPTURE

Read the story of Jesus' anointing in John 12:1–8. Remember that if the primary mode of transportation in that day was walking, his feet must've grown mighty tired and sore. Think how Jesus, so fully human, so sensitive and keenly alert, must've delighted in the woman's touch, the scent of her perfume, the silky feel of hair and ointment on his feet. What does his experience of touch tell us about our experiences of touch?

PAUSE TO REFLECT

- Remember a time when touch communicated more than words. What was the message?

- Do you believe our touch can convey God's healing comfort? Why or why not?

STOP FOR A MOMENT

Another moment to pause and savor our progress. We're halfway through this forty-step adventure in faith and art, slowly but surely seeing ourselves, others, the world, and even God with new eyes. Look back over the first half of this book and draw two or three conclusions for yourself from what you've done so far.

YOUR THOUGHTS

_____

_____

_____

_____

_____

_____

_____

_____

_____

_____

_____

_____

_____

step 21

Faith as a Wrestling Act

As we said in Step 2: The Foundations, the greatest thinkers who ever lived wrestled with the same issues we do. Some people just hunker down and try to endure the tough parts. Others make a prodigious effort to understand and communicate their insights. It's the latter group we're interested in here. Through the arts, we can share in their struggle.

Imagine, for a moment, that you are dying. You have a chance to leave a last message. You struggle to put together a few short words. What do you say?

We know from the cell phone messages left by those who died on 9/11 that few people wasted time on "pay the bills" or "punish that nasty neighbor." Instead, most contained words of love. The moral for the rest of us: when time is short, focus on the positive.

At the last supper, Jesus faced the same thing. He knew his time with his friends was short. Facing a certain expiration date, he wanted to communicate what he most wanted them to remember. So he said: I am leaving you, but you won't be alone. I will remain with you. Remember "Hill St. Blues," the television show about cops facing danger daily? Like their sergeant, Jesus knew the ugly, violent, fearsome world his friends faced. So in similar words, he said, "Be careful out there."

He warned his friends in John 16: the forces of evil will appear to triumph, you'll be kicked out of the synagogues, lose everything that is most precious, and those who kill you will be proud that their murderous deed pleases God. In contemporary expression, he said, "The dark is rising."

It's enough to make any smart person run screaming in the other direction. "It's been nice hanging out with you, Jesus. And those were some nifty cures. But I've got a family to look out for." The legitimate, unspoken response would've been, "If what you predict is really coming, I've got to protect my own hide. I'm outta here!" The natural instinct would've been to "vote with one's feet."

But Jesus' message must've been persuasive. After Judas' departure, when Jesus speaks most directly, no one else leaves. His words are filled with the tenderness of a parent who must tell a child bad news. His yearning to remain with them beyond death is so intense, it becomes a person: the Spirit. "I will ask the Father, and he will give you another Advocate, to be with you for ever" (John 14:16).

He asks them, then, to trust his promise. From the last supper discourse we get a clear picture: faith isn't a matter of following rules, but of abiding in trust. Nor does belief in God offer any protection or guaranteed escape from horrifying ordeals. The tragedies will come, Jesus assures them. But I'll be with you through them.

A woman facing cancer writes of making this insight her own. She staggers through diagnosis and treatment, terrified of the dark, unable to sleep. With a malignancy eating away at her core, there is nothing she can do. Through a long wrestling match, she comes to realize that God never promised to take away suffering or death, but to stay with us through it.

The prayer into which she finally relaxes comes from Scripture: "It is I. Be not afraid." "It is I. I am also at the center of all that you most fear. There is no otherness. It is I." It made her see that while she would do everything possible to have the cancer treated, it was not alien to God. Her disease didn't exist "in a land that God could not visit" (Margaret Macey, "When Light Yields to Darkness," *America*, May 29, 2006, 22).

It may be the hardest struggle we ever face: integrating faith with our worst experiences. But God is one, remaining present in everything. It also helps to know we aren't the first to wrestle. A long line of thinkers and wrestlers precedes us, and fortunately, they have left us finely wrought final words, images, and music.

RELEVANT QUOTES

There is always a moment in any kind of struggle
when one feels in full bloom.
Vivid.
Alive.
One might be blown to bits in such a moment,
  and still be at peace...
To be such a person or to witness anyone
at this moment of transcendent presence is to know
that what is human is linked, by daring compassion,
to what is divine.

During my years of being close to people engaged
in changing the world, I have seen
fear turn into courage;
sorrow into joy;
funerals into celebrations.

Because whatever the consequences,
people, standing side by side,
have expressed who they are, and that ultimately
they believe in the love of the world
and in each other....
—ALICE WALKER, *Anything We Love Can Be Saved*
(NEW YORK: BALLANTINE BOOKS, 1997)

Although the world is full of suffering, it is full also of the over-coming of it.
—HELEN KELLER

Never to suffer would never to have been blessed.
—EDGAR ALLAN POE

PAUSE TO REFLECT

- What problem do you wrestle with most right now?

SCRIPTURE

Read slowly through John 16. What does Jesus seem to be saying to his friends, and hence to you? Do you find anything there that might help with the current dilemma?

YOUR THOUGHTS

_____

_____

_____

_____

_____

The Art of Dance

Then the prophet Miriam, Aaron's sister, took a tambourine in her hand; and all the women went out after her with tambourines and with dancing. EXODUS 15:20

In step twenty-two we turn to the dance. There's hope even if you dance only at a wedding to understand dance as a larger metaphor for the life of faith. Early Christians called the inner circle of the Trinity *perichoeresis,* or "dancing around."

William Barry, SJ, adds, "We need to think of music and dance and words together as a symbol of the inner life of God," the ground of our universe. He continues, "At every moment of existence we are being drawn by the music of this eternal dance to become conscious participants in it. God wants us to be partners in the dance, to be so intimate that we share the inner life of the Trinity" (Foreword to Kathy Coffey, *God in the Moment,* Chicago: Loyola Press, 1999, ix).

Others refer to the Trinity as engaged in constant dialogue, which must be as beautiful as strings singing to woodwinds in a symphony or as lilting as Irish voices. While we might be able to imagine the three persons engaged in some Welsh song-fest, it's harder to picture ourselves joining the chorus—or partnering in the dance.

Yet we have moments that give us a glimpse—when all our powers are in high gear, emotions, minds, and bodies alert, hearts aflame, gifts all channeled into one rhythm. It may come as we summit a mountain peak, complete a marathon, birth a baby or a project, sink into beauty, fall in love or stay there, rejoice with a friend or relative, absorb a lovely place, bite into a celebratory meal, exult in being who we are, exactly as we are.

At such times, we realize that we could never have done as much as we have done alone, with human limits. God is our partner in the dance, bowing to us and offering a hand. If it helps, imagine God as the king approaching Anna for a waltz in *The King and I.* "Shall we dance?" asks God. And for three beats, we hesitate. Then scooping up a skirt, we're off on rollicking, rhythmic, fluid movement. (This of course, is the female viewpoint. But for a male it must be equally daring and exciting when he approaches the woman he has admired from afar, and she agrees to dance with him.)

To take that first step onto the dance floor is in itself a risk. We must trust ourselves and the partner, who is often unknown. We are then swept into a larger music we can't control. Often not knowing the specific steps, we improvise. We count on the body to catch the beat and move to the rhythm. And if we are fortunate, the partner is compassionate, subtly guiding us so we don't look klutzy.

It's all a bit like tightrope walking. What gives us courage to do it is the rest of the group, clearly having more fun on the floor than the crew that's hugging the punch bowl.

Some of the finest dance springs from people who have been oppressed: the South Africans, the Irish. White people may hold the privileges in the U.S., but African Americans, long denied basic rights, lead the way in dance. Dancing, unlike writing or painting, doesn't require equipment: simply a body and a tune we can sing ourselves. Like many of life's best things (a sunset, a meadow, a mountain), it's free, hence free from power.

For most people, dance is purely celebratory, unlike sports where we compete or try to get in shape. The song pours over us, the beat pulses through us and we respond. As in life, we learn new steps, stumble, and sometimes look awkward—but the dance goes on. And it needn't be in a ballroom; sometimes we dance for joy in the kitchen or near the phone where we heard good news. We may not be graceful, but we're full of good intentions!

The professional dancer reverences the miracles of small bones in wrists and feet, with their vast repetoire of movement. A ballerina has trained the body to take full advantage of its remarkable range. So too the faithful person trusts in the equipment God has provided for whatever their task might be. They know this God-partner whom they cannot see. So they can turn over life in trust, moving wherever and however God leads.

This may seem too romantic, overlooking the hard practice which undergirds every art. But dancer Martha Graham sees the practice itself as an act of vision, hope, and desire. She says, "I think the reason dance has held such an ageless magic for the world is that it has been the symbol of the performance of living....One becomes in some area an athlete of God" ("I Am a Dancer," in Diane Apostolos-Cappadona and Lucinda Ebersole, eds. *Women, Creativity, and the Arts*, New York: Continuum, 1995, 145).

Nelson Mandela once said, "Never put a gun in the hand of a man who doesn't dance." He must have meant, "You can't entrust life to someone who doesn't know it at its best—graceful, melodic, and beauteous."

RELEVANT QUOTES

The cosmic dance beats in our very blood.

—THOMAS MERTON

There is one Great Being who enlivens the dance of our beautiful planet and everything that exists. The darkness of outer space, the greenness of our land and the blue of our seas, the breath of every human and creature, all are intimately united in a cosmic dance of oneness with the Creator's breath of love.

—JOYCE RUPP, *The Cosmic Dance*

POEM

IRISH DANCER, AGE 10

She bows.
   one black-gloved leg extended
   hair tumultuous over green band
   cape hung with Tara's crests.

Then the sparrows of her feet
carry conversation
with bagpipes clothed in plaid.

She dances
   but it is not she:
   her great-grandmothers carved
   ancestral patterns which transcend one dancer.

No confusion snares her.
Straight-shouldered, she moves in grace
that is tradition's birthright.

Flushed, she bows.
   exchanges her costume for jeans
   returns to dissonant suburbia
   the dance her passport to greener space.

The Art of Gardening

And the Lord God planted a garden in Eden, in the east; and there
he put the man whom he had formed. Out of the ground the Lord
God made to grow every tree that is pleasant to the sight and good
for food.
  They heard the sound of the Lord God walking in the garden at
the time of the evening breeze.... GENESIS 2:8–9, 3:8

Those who garden are artists who create growing, fragrant tapes-
tries. The rest of us admire gardeners from afar, doubting we could
persist through weeding and watering in hot July.

  An easy way for the non-gardener to appreciate the gardener's
art is to stroll through local parks or gardens. Admiring the flower
beds becomes a ritual way to mark the passage of summer.

  We flower-nuts pouring into the gardens are a mild lot, the gen-
tly-obsessed. We simply like the graceful way Queen Ann's lace
floats, a dragonfly pivots faster than a blink, or a bowl of water lily
holds the light. We don't come only for the exotic—the black
pansy, the allium which looks like a bursting bulb of fireworks. We
like the steady, quiet growth, the baby ducks growing from puff-
balls into mature, wage-earning, tax-paying ducks.

In June, the first flowering is a burst of joy, a pirouette after the final curtain on winter. The heart does flip-flops at every turn of the path: peonies! roses! iris! Spring is slow in coming to the Rocky Mountains but when it does, stand back! Texture, color and smell almost overwhelm.

After rain the night before, drops balance artfully on the full, plump roses. Pastel balls swirl like dancers' skirts. In the aftermath of rain, some areas smell like the mountains, piney and rich. Down these elegant pathways lined with fountains and flowers, one should walk in a ballgown, swish in silk.

By July, less overwhelmed, I can be more attentive to details. The verbena I'd previously known only in red surprises in purple and burgundy. The bacopa grown at home in white and lavender blooms here in a coral called "African sunset." A second wave of roses blossoms in intriguing colors: spackled fushia and white, or golden globes like Julian of Norwich saw the world, a walnut in God's hand. What a profound effect it has on the soul, this sustained immersion in beauty.

Italian author Piero Ferrucci writes in *What We May Be:*

the moment we let ourselves be touched by beauty, that part of us which has been badly bruised or even shattered by the events of life may begin to be revitalized. At that moment a true victory takes place—a victory over discouragement....That victory is also a step forward in our growth...for the moment we fully appreciate beauty, we become more than we were. We live a moment of pure psychological health. (188)

The realist would quickly point out that this garden exists in the midst of a crazed world, that traffic roars outside its gates, where people suffer horribly and die. To be convincing, any theory of beauty must spring from the garden of good and evil or it risks being sentimental.

Times in the garden are for me times of prayer. Absorbed in beauty, I poke my nose into anything that might smell good. I wear an outrageous straw hat with a pink gingham bow that I wouldn't be caught dead in anywhere else. This delight in the variety of God's creation leaves me spunkier, calmer, more generous. In the garden when we rest from more serious work, we can be what we most deeply are: perfumed beauty, God's delight.

PAUSE TO REFLECT

- Have you ever felt as the author does about the beauty of a garden? If so, describe your feeling.

- If you *are* a gardener, describe what it means to create such short-lived beauty.

- If the goal of art is to bring us to prayer and praise, making us kinder and more generous, then the garden succeeds. What other ways have you been brought into the prayerful state this garden visit achieved?

SCRIPTURE

Jesus could have chosen any place for his resurrection. Yet John records: "Now there was a garden in the place where he was crucified, and in the garden there was a new tomb in which no one had ever been laid." (19:41) Jesus is buried in a garden, where the never-seen-before surge of resurrected life splits open the tomb.

And why does Mary Magdalene make the mistake she does? "Supposing him to be the gardener…" (20:15). It's certainly understandable: after a sleepless, tear-filled night, she was probably bleary-eyed. But she could've mistaken him for a soldier, a merchant, or a shepherd out for an early morning stroll. Her mistake becomes wonderfully symbolic: she identifies Jesus with all who bring new life, color, fragrance, texture, and sweetness into our world.

Next time a gardener is sweating through a particularly weedy patch, or surveying the peonies with special pride, he or she should remember: Jesus was once thought to be a gardener, too.

RELEVANT QUOTES

How lovely is the silence of growing things.
—GARDENER'S PLAQUE

If a man wants to be happy for a week, he should take a wife; if he wants to be happy for a month, he should kill a pig, but if he desires happiness forever, he should plant a garden.
—ANCIENT CHINESE SAYING

For the flowers are great blessings,
For the Lord made a nosegay in the meadow with his disciples and preached upon the lily…
For flowers are good both for the living and the dead.
For there is a language of flowers…
For elegant phrases are nothing but flowers…
For the Poorman's nosegay is an introduction to a Prince…
—CHRISTOPHER SMART

YOUR THOUGHTS

_____

_____

_____

_____

_____

The Art of Poetry

The day after the tragedy of 9/11 (how sad that all recognize the shorthand), I happened to be in Washington, DC, with a free afternoon. I used that time to visit the National Gallery, which had hastily assembled a brief security screening. After that harsh reminder of new realities, I joined a tour, which the guide began by saying, "The works in this museum have endured through countless wars, acts of terrorism, plagues, bloodbaths, and other horrors of history. They show that something in the human spirit is better, longer-lived than all the violence. And that's what endures today."

Keeping her words in mind, I looked at the paintings as if they were a treasure house of the human spirit. She was right: the dew on peaches painted in the seventeenth century still sparkled. The skin of nineteenth-century models still blushed. The dawn rose over peaks in Yosemite, Rouen Cathedral, or the Thames River as if it were here today.

This experience with the visual arts prompted me to think about my favorite art, poetry, and how it endures. For me, it is most directly linked to faith. A dancer once explained that she didn't do liturgical dance because it was a cute or showy performance. It was the most dignified movement she could do that best gave glory to God.

Poetry is the best of any language; there is only a shadowy, permeable boundary between it and prayer. Indeed, many who cannot use official forms of prayer find poetry expresses their longing for God. Poet Galway Kinnell once called it "the life with the most life in it." While that may sound like a beer commercial, it represents the surge of the fullest life available to limited human beings. It comes close to what Jesus must have meant when he said, "I came that you might have life and have it in abundance."

Poetry began in religious rituals. Throughout history, writing and hearing poetry have been considered religious acts. At the beginning of an epic poem such as *The Iliad* or *The Odyssey*, ancient Greek poets invoked the Muse, the god of inspiration. Ancient Celtic people held poets in high esteem as magicians and seers.

What makes poetry unique among the arts? Experts will answer in different ways, so this is a purely personal response. It stems from many years of loving poetry and connecting it to faith.

• Poetry comes as close as we humans can to immortality. Like the other arts, it contains eternal truths. But poetry for me is the most precise expression of the emotions and experiences many of us struggle to articulate. Because of this precision and universality, I can still be stirred by insights from another century or another era. The seventh-century Asian poet's love for his deceased wife still moves me in the twenty-first century. We live in the same world, with its seasons, tastes, loves, hatreds, losses, mountains, and seas. Poets of all times and places help me appreciate it.

If, as many believe, a large part of faith is gratitude, poets who celebrate the human condition increase my thankfulness for having this time on earth. However limited it may be, there is much in life to celebrate. Furthermore, poetry inspires an imaginative movement beyond the boundaries of the self, a step toward compassion. Jesus encourages this empathy with another person's experience but doesn't always spell out how to get there. Poetry helps.

• Poetry is the proper form for celebration. Its language comes as close as we can to reaching the divine. No one places a rare brandy in a cracked old Coke bottle. So too, poetic language is the finest vessel for praise, like a Waterford crystal decanter. Sometimes our emotions burst the seams of prose; we can't be restricted by the usual syntax. That's when we branch into poetry, as if we were taking flight.

• Jesus holds a perennial appeal for poets. Across the world and across the centuries, they have been intrigued by him and have portrayed him with endless variations. If he is, as Christians believe, the central figure of our faith, then we turn to poetry eagerly, to find fresh aspects of his character. To break open our numb familiarity, we need bold, disarming poetry. Often it surprises, because it is invitational, playful, never preachy.

Poem

Consecration

Anne Sexton should be here now.
"I plead with it to be true," she wrote.
"Even if I can't believe it,
I plead with it to be true."
At this Eucharist, it was.

The curved parentheses
of Kevin's hands cupped
a reckless grace.
His buoyant gesture shaped
perfect poetry:

we could blaze with God
(even the doubters, Anne)
as bread could turn to body
and cup could hold
the burgundy of blood.

RELEVANT QUOTES

Poetry is the flowering of ordinary possibilities.

—THOMAS MERTON

To transform the outrage of the years
Into a music, a rumor and a symbol,
To see in death a sleep, and in the sunset
A sad gold, of such is Poetry....

—JORGE LUIS BORGES

God needs prophets in order to make himself known, and all prophets are necessarily artistic. What a prophet has to say can never be said in prose.

—HANS URS VON BALTHASAR

It is difficult
to get the news from poems
yet men die miserably every day
for lack
of what is found there.

—WILLIAM CARLOS WILLIAMS

The reader of poetry is a kind of pilgrim setting out, setting forth....Reading poetry is an adventure in renewal, a creative act, a perpetual beginning, a rebirth of wonder.

—EDWARD HIRSCH

Poetry points us to "that more radiant and generous life which the imagination desires."

—SEAMUS HEANEY

PAUSE TO REFLECT

- How do you feel about poetry? To what extent does it enrich your faith?

step 25

Making Mantras

Set me like a seal on your heart, like a seal on your arm.

SONG OF SONGS 8:6

I have carved you on the palm of my hand. ISAIAH 49:16

So all this theory is nice, but what are some practical steps toward the art of faith? One step that a spiritual director suggested has been helpful to me. She was a splendid woman who suffered from insomnia. One way she coped with sleepless nights was by creating seven-syllable mantras, then repeating them until they eventually soothed her to sleep. The word *mantra* comes from the Hindu, meaning "a word or formula chanted or sung as an incantation or prayer."

The mantra helps heal not only insomnia, but also stress. In a tense situation, it reminds us, "this too will pass." Whatever the stress is, it doesn't change the most basic things about us: we belong to God. In God's plan, nothing can permanently harm us. Christ has died for us and lives in us: what more could we want?

The problem is, few people think of theology during a blizzard, major appliance breakdown, dentist appointment, traffic jam, biopsy or airport delay. But at the times we are frightened and frustrated, we most need a reminder that we're not in this alone. God, constant companion and friend, is with us. If we have mantras on hand, we simply repeat one steadily, breathing deeply. Without intense thought or formulas from a book, we invite God into wherever we are. We might begin with biblical texts, adapted to the seven-syllable mold:

I will not leave you orphaned.

Many rooms in Father's house.

House of prayer, not den of thieves.

I am with you 'til the end.

Worth more than many sparrows.

Say but the word; I'll be healed.

No one takes away your joy.

Your name will be Beloved.

The kingdom of God is near.

This is my body, for you.

This is the cup of my blood.

Do this and remember me.

Images of intimate resting in God appear throughout John's gospel. Just as Jesus abides in the Father, so John (the stand-in for us all) sits next to Jesus at the last supper (John 13:23) and leans into him. The word for abide or rest (*meno*) occurs frequently; the word for pray or prayer never does in John. That interesting theological nugget is captured in the mantra: "*Rest in God still; rest in me*" or "*Where I am, you may be too.*"

One morning I read Jesus' question to his disciples, which also falls handily into seven syllables: *Who do you say that I am?* That question ran silently beneath the day's activities. When I became anxious that I could never squeeze in everything I'd planned, I'd repeat the mantra. Surely if I believed that God had created the universe, mountains, and stars, God could handle one tight schedule. When I encountered the unexpected delight of window boxes flowering colorfully against creamy stucco walls, I remembered the mantra and added a dimension: *You are the source of beauty.*

Even mantras without a scriptural base can hold deep spiritual truths: *God in each beat of my heart. Beloved, I trust in you. Hold me (or Name) in your loving arms. I'm never really alone. No anxiety today. In each new moment, beauty. So much happiness today. I live in lavish blessing. God shapes my life artfully.*

Looking back through my journal, I can trace the course of a year through the mantras recorded there. On New Year's Day, looking back over a year of travel, friends' visits, a root canal, work, parties, a skin cancer removed, beaches, boredom, the mantra was an attempt to summarize: *Enter it all and bless it. Surrounded by love and grace* marked a day of skiing through deep powder. Frequently anticipating visits from my children, I'd sprinkle the journal with: *I'll see my kids tomorrow* or *Beloved daughter is home.* Anyone can fill in the blank: *My friend (Name) is here today.* Insomniacs who, like my director, suffer from sleepless nights then finally sleeps, can acknowledge that blessing with a mantra: *Deep sleep on clean sheets. Thank you.* It's the ultimate reassurance to someone who's sick or young or afraid: *I'll be here when you wake up.*

A homilist tells of the common practice among students of writing important information on their hands. While often this is an assignment deadline or a phone number, sometimes it's more profound.

One girl came to see a school counselor about a painful breakup with her first love, a genuine heart-break at age sixteen. The counselor noticed blue marks on her arm and worried that these might violate a school rule prohibiting tattoos.

"Oh, no!" the girl replied, horrified. "I copied a line that's important to me right now: '*Don't let it overcome you.*'" Seven syllables became her life raft through emotional crisis. Throughout a lifetime, the meaning of "it" might change, but the mantra reminded her she was larger than any particular obstacle and could draw on spiritual resources to withstand life's successive blows.

PAUSE TO REFLECT

- "Don't let it overcome you." What's the "it" in your life right now? Financial insecurity? Anger? Fear? Illness? A problem with a relationship or work? If you could write a few words of encouragement on your hand to help survive this crisis, what would they be?

- On the palm of God's hand is written your name. How do you feel about that?

- Of all the scriptural mantras listed, which one seems best fitted for you right now?

ACTION SUGGESTION

Use one of the suggested mantras this week, when you're caught in traffic, lying awake at night, or showering. Then create your own mantra, drawn from the Bible, a favorite line of poetry, or the current circumstances of your life. Count the seven syllables of the words on your fingers.

YOUR THOUGHTS

_____

_____

_____

_____

_____

The Art of Weaving

I'm no expert at actual weaving. The one time I watched a Navajo weaver, I realized I'd run away screaming if I had to spend hours creating an inch. What I mean by weaving in the spiritual sense is closer to the Michael Joncas song, "We Come to Your Feast," which mentions "the weaving of our stories, the fabric of our lives." The art lies in creating a coherent whole. We weave together what we know of Jesus, modern art and science, our present life experience and environment, memories and relationships.

How can we be attentive and reflective, knowledgeable and pro-foundly grateful—all at once? As every religious tradition has taught, experience must be framed by white spaces of quiet. Anyone working intently on a project knows how the challenges of organizing, expressing, finding enough time, not letting length or complexity overwhelm, getting a handle on all the pieces can lead to teeth-gnashing frustration. Yet time away—a weekend breather or even a good night's sleep—makes a huge difference.

We return re-energized, able to see with fresh perspective. Driving away from the mountains sometimes enables us to see them more clearly than we can when surrounded by them. So too with the artful life: the pauses in the music, like the frames around the art, enhance the whole.

When my children were small, we once discovered in a forest a super-sized spider web. It was a stunning design, bejeweled with dew, and for a long time, we simply observed it, awed. That shining web serves as a metaphor for the inter-connections we can make and the joy of seeing how they relate to each other. A cherished memory can be awakened by revisiting the site where it first occurred—or even smelling a particular fragrance again: the smell of the sea or lavender or tobacco.

One example of weaving science and Scripture is that psychologists say that ninety percent of what we worry about will never happen. Where have we heard that before? "Do not let your hearts be troubled" (John 14:1).

JESUS, THE ARTFUL WEAVER

Surely one challenge that confronts all thinking Christians is weaving a relationship with their religious tradition. They question the role of law within their heritage and within their own lives. If someone hasn't wrestled with the rules or become frustrated by the failures of institutions, one wonders what planet they've been grazing on lately.

In this as in all puzzles, we turn to Jesus, the artful weaver. He boldly named the hypocrisy of synagogue officials: "whitened sepulchers." The name has stuck because it calls up such a vivid image: behind the slick surface, rotting, putrid corpses.

Jesus' attitude toward the law reveals a healthy balance. On one hand, he respects the scrolls read in the synagogue and tells the people that Isaiah is "fulfilled in your hearing," through him. On the other, he points out, "The Sabbath was made for man, not man for the Sabbath." He ignored customs such as repeated hand washing, and cured people and picked grain on the sabbath.

His position comes down to this: if the rule serves the person, honor it. If, on the other hand, it demeans or impoverishes God's beloved creature, ignore it. God always desires fullness of life and abiding joy for God's child. Jesus cut through the bewildering thicket of Jewish laws by focusing on the great commandments: Love God. Love each other. The rest is detail.

Most of us work a lifetime to learn to follow that "Golden Rule." We weave together various approaches to church teaching: sometimes questioning, sometimes agreeing, always seeking to become more Christ-like and to follow Christ more closely.

It helps to place our efforts within a larger design. God cares for and protects us more than we ever dream. Sometimes the threads of our attempts come together with astonishing elegance. Sometimes we fail, and the tapestry is torn. But always we are in the skilled hands of a Master Weaver who blesses our individual weaving with beauty and strength.

RELEVANT QUOTES

You need only claim the events of your life to make yourself yours. When you truly possess all you have been and done…you are fierce with reality. —FLORIDA SCOTT MAXWELL

PAUSE TO REFLECT

- "Frame" yesterday's experience with quiet time. Where in that day was God most present/absent? What was God trying to tell you through the people you met, the surprises, the work you did, the accomplishments, graces, failures, disappointments, or fun? (All speak eloquently, so don't gloss over the negative—or the positive.)

- What was a connection you made recently between various parts of your life—perhaps between an event and a memory, or between lived experience and Scripture, or between something you read and something you learned in conversation?

ACTION SUGGESTION

Take a break from whatever you're doing today. Try the pleasant British pause for a "cuppa," religiously observed every afternoon. For you, tea may not do the trick but you know yourself well enough to know what refreshes: a walk outdoors? music? prayer? exercise? a nap? a snack? a stretch? a conversation? doing nothing? Then analyze the difference on your return to routine. Did the pause refresh enough to make it a regular practice?

YOUR THOUGHTS

_____

_____

_____

_____

_____

_____

_____

_____

_____

_____

step 27

Singing Our Sadness

The reading of the passion at our parish is punctuated by a song from David Haas:

> We hold the death of the Lord
> Deep in our hearts. Living, now
> We remain with Jesus the Christ.

Life is tough—for everyone, no matter how we seem to have it all together. What carries us through the rough parts? Music, poetry, beauty, community, a sense of meaning. These elements come together in good liturgy.

The weaving of Scripture with song becomes like a tinted window through which we see Christ's passion, and Christ's passion in turn interprets our experience. Two pews ahead of me sits a couple whose daughter died recently at age twenty-four of a massive infection. She was a buoyant, vivacious girl—in her and in her parents' grief, Christ dies again. Next to me sits a dear friend from college days. Divorced thirteen years ago, she struggles with raising her five children, finding a path toward financial security.

Two pews behind me, they lean together as they sing: a couple who have survived various forms of cancer. They continue their generous ministries in a weakened but still vibrant old age. A widow with young children looks overwhelmed; even those who appear happy and healthy bear secret sorrows which weigh on their shoulders like crosses. And this parish is only one of many throughout the world where people learn to find meaning in suffering.

It goes on and on, the passion of Christ lived out in more ways than one human could ever experience. Pilate's interrogation occurs at juvenile court in Seattle; the torture chambers in Jerusalem move to Iraq; Judas' kiss betrays the pregnant Danish teen when the father of her child disappears; the sad story is enacted again and again in a Santiago parish.

When we memorialize the passion, we let the power of the original story wash over us, touch us, soak into us. The deeper we enter the story, the more the story enters us. We read the same events in Jesus' life each year with a slightly different lens, which comes from the events we've lived through that year.

What defeats us, scholars say, isn't suffering, but meaningless suffering. We can endure the ordeal if we see some value in it, place our pain in solidarity with Jesus' and others who suffer around the world. And when we are too frail, too tired, or too lost to comprehend what's going on, the community carries us. We count on them to keep singing its refrain, reminding us that we are united to the suffering Christ. All that horrifies us—aging, disease, poverty, war—has some ultimate connection to the source of all good. If there is an art to suffering, perhaps it lies in joining ours with Christ's.

Our suffering isn't occasioned only by death, but sometimes by the gap between where we are and where we'd like to be. I once lamented the use of the song "All Are Welcome" to a musician friend. The lyrics proclaim more a dream than a reality. In fact, all are not welcome in many churches. Then my friend reminded me, "Sometimes we need to sing ourselves into the place where we should be."

So we'll sing the Haas refrain over and over. Maybe someday we'll get it right. We'll live it.

PAUSE TO REFLECT

- What song has had the kind of meaning for you which the author describes?

ACTION SUGGESTION

Next time you're suffering, try singing your favorite song quietly to yourself.

RELEVANT QUOTE

The author of this ancient homily on Holy Saturday imagines Christ speaking:

"Rise up, work of my hands, you who were created in my image. Rise, let us leave this place, for you are in me and I am in you; together we form only one person and we cannot be separated."
—LITURGY OF THE HOURS, 1976, 497

YOUR THOUGHTS

_____

_____

_____

_____

_____

_____

The Art of Music

I write as a non-musician, which may prompt sneers from the musicians and relief from those as clueless as I. While I do not know the history of great composers, how to sing harmony, or how to write music, I do appreciate it. I know first-hand how music can affect daily life, just as it can change the mood in a movie.

Attending a concert where Respighi's "Pines of the Appian Way" was performed, the audience was suddenly surrounded by the orchestra. Trumpeters appeared in the balconies and drummers in the aisles. The steady thrumming grew louder, more insistent. And we were transported to Italy as Caesar's army marched. All this transpired without buying a plane ticket or packing a suitcase: instant travel through time and space, through music. Like the colors in a painting, musical tones can evoke the whole range of human emotion, from heavy mourning to exultant joy, from calm to agitation, from restlessness to deep peace.

Like any art form, music can hold the light and the dark. Steve Warner, director of the Notre Dame folk choir, comments on how music conveys both to his students:

> If I don't pass on to them and help them appreciate the depth
> of what our hymns are, the theology in them, I'm setting them

up for parochial failure once they leave the university. Young adults need not only to be joyful but to learn how to lament. If we choose pop music to give to young adults, we don't teach them how to grieve, and that despair, as well as joy, is a necessary part of the landscape of our faith. (quoted in Renee LaReau, "Uncommon Choir," *National Catholic Reporter*, July 28, 2006, 13)

Through the minor miracle of the iPod, music can be carried where we need it most. In my pocket I can hold a symphony—or a blast of the Beatles.

After a meeting in which my confidence in a project was badly shaken, I once took a walk with Handel. The thrilling notes of his *Water Music* restored my better self. Walking through high alpine desert, I heard the splash of oars along the Thames. Wearing jogging shorts and a t-shirt, I heard the swish of satin and brocade as people in elegant costumes processed. Feeling small, I regained my royal dignity.

Sitting beside a lily pond, I listened to "Jesu, Joy of Man's Desiring." The music soared like light over pastel flowers. I wanted to rest in God as the lilies rested like floating cups in the lake. The scene symbolized the Christian community, too. All of us together bear different colors like lanterns swimming in the dark. A church member interviewed by Robert Wuthnow said, "Sometimes when we're singing and the spirit is moving, it's almost like the roof goes away and you can see the heavens. When we're all in sync, you can feel the spirit moving."

I return to the beauty of music as the struggles of the week emerge: a balky co-worker, tedious chores, a wounded and meddlesome acquaintance, a stressful deadline, a honking traffic jam, too little time with the people I love, too much with those I'd rather avoid. Beneath it all can run the lovely lines of Bach. Silently I hum his melody.

If we ever doubt the importance of music, we should gauge our reaction when a favorite song is sung badly or a piece we love is interrupted. "Don't mess with Pachelbel!" I once wanted to growl at an inept CD-meister who kept halting the concerto abruptly.

Music probably began as a religious act to accompany ritual. It continues to play a vital role in the life of faith. Within worship, it sustains us when a service grows dull, and teaches profound truths enjoyably. It persuades people to believe truths that might be harder to believe without music, such as:

- Together, we can transform this world.
  Let us build the City of God
  May our tears be turned into dancing
  For our Lord, our light and our love,
  Has turned the dark into day. ("City of God," by Dan Schutte)
- We are brothers and sisters with millions of people who speak different languages.
  We are one body, the body of Christ
  and we do not stand alone. (sung by millions of teenagers at World Youth Day in Denver, 1993)
- Something in human beings survives death.
  Doubtful? Yet we sing at funerals "May the Angels Lead You into Paradise," "On Eagle's Wings" or "We Shall Find an Open Door."

The persuasive powers of music in a worship setting shouldn't be so surprising. After all, gospel songs helped slaves endure a horrific ordeal, military marches sent people into battle, jeopardizing their lives, folk songs convinced settlers to build each other's barns. Singing in worship releases endorphins that are not released in any other setting.

As I often remind my friends who give sermons: "No one goes home humming the homily." The music of liturgy stretches our spirits. The extent to which music is woven into our souls is indicated by a story about a Southern Baptist woman who had many disagreements with her tradition. Finally she realized: "I'd love to stop being a Southern Baptist but I'd have to forget too many songs." The music had seeped into the core of her being.

RELEVANT QUOTES

Ah, music. A magic beyond all we do here! —J.K. ROWLING

Music is the only language in which you cannot say a mean or sarcastic thing. —JOHN ERSKINE

SCRIPTURE

This psalm captures the pain of exile through a meaningful metaphor, the loss of a peoples' treasured music.

> By the rivers of Babylon—
>   there we sat down and there we wept
>   when we remembered Zion.
> On the willows there
>   we hung up our harps.
> For there our captors
>   asked us for songs,
> and our tormentors asked for mirth, saying,
>   "Sing us one of the songs of Zion!"
> How could we sing the Lord's song
>   in a foreign land?

—PSALM 137:1–4

The Art of Cooking

She moves through a kitchen like a queen. Skilled and confident, she tweaks a meringue here, deftly cracks an egg there. The meals she assembles, apparently without effort, are works of art: textures, fragrances, tastes, and colors combine on a plate as if it were a palette. She works with fresh fruits and vegetables as if they were the instruments in an orchestra or shades of oil paint.

She has become the matriarch of a large clan; many generations of nieces, nephews, and grandchildren revolve like spokes of a wheel around her center. Where else would they want to go? Her home is their haven; the table its centerpiece. When she speaks of a family dinner or a favorite recipe, her eyes fill with light. What's the best cure for a cranky adolescent or a brooding great uncle? She pulls out the pan for cinnamon rolls.

Good cooks stand within a long tradition. Compliment a chef, and she'll humbly nod to a mother or mentor who preceded her. "Oh, my spaghetti sauce doesn't hold a candle to my mom's!" he'll demur. The act of cooking seems to kindle memories.

One metaphor that recurs throughout Scripture is that life itself is an abundant meal, cooked with the lavish, creative generosity of

God. When God invites us, "Come to the feast!" we know we're in for some "fine eatin'."

When Jesus nourished 5000 (John 6:5–13), the scene moves from scarcity to abundance. The story begins with the set-up: when the disciples say no one could feed such a crowd, they cue Jesus to surprise. He feeds huge numbers with five barley loaves and two fish. One phrase is key: they ate "as much as they wanted."

Anyone who's ever been a nervous chef, wondering if there's enough, knows the importance of that phrase. Anyone who's ever been a child in a large, grabby family knows what a relief it is to be satisfied. Even better: there were leftovers. One delight of a dinner party is raiding the refrigerator the next day. All those goodies, and no one has to cook! Scarcity and abundance stand in sharp contrast, and God offers plenty of the nurture we really need.

RELEVANT QUOTES

If more of us valued food and cheer and song above hoarded gold, it would be a merrier world. —J.R.R. TOLKIEN

One good deed is better than three days of fasting. —JAPANESE PROVERB

Cooking is at once child's play and adult joy. And cooking done with care is an act of love. —CRAIG CLAIBORNE

Sharing food with another human being is an intimate act that should not be indulged in lightly. —M.F.K. FISHER

Good food ends with good talk. —GEOFFREY NEIGHBOR

Remember a meal now

What made it special? Perhaps it was the person who sat across the table from us. If so, imagine looking deep into God's eyes and finding there the same spark, magnified. Or was it the setting? Did the table overlook a green valley, a lake, a fireplace, an ocean, a mountain range, a familiar neighborhood? Picture your favorite table: outdoors with a checkered cloth, or in a beautiful room with sparkling crystal, china, soft linen. Now imagine that table moved to the eternal kingdom of justice and peace.

Maybe the food was special: what are your favorite dishes? Were they served? Did ice cream top hot apple pie? Did the froth of latte overflow a hand-painted cup? Did the aroma of steak predict it would melt in your mouth? Or was the fish caught this morning in an adjoining lake? Was the butter sliding across ears of corn fresh from the field? Whatever the food, intensify its flavor, subtract its calories, and picture it in quantities that never end, never spoil nor satiate. Now you've gotten a glimpse of the unending feast God's cooking up for you.

Prayer

For food in a world where many walk in hunger
For friends in a world where many walk alone
For faith in a world where many walk in fear
We give you thanks, O Lord.

—Anglican Church of Canada

Scripture

The Jewish/Christian tradition is rich in accounts of shared meals. A smorgasbord of stories: Abraham and Sarah entertaining angels, (Genesis 18:1–15) Martha, patron saint of chefs (Luke 10:38–42), the last supper (Matthew 26:20–30; John 13:1–16).

Pause to reflect

- It's not a huge leap of the imagination to compare the banquet God hosts in life with the best meals we've enjoyed. Savor in memory a recent, excellent meal. What did you eat? Drink? How did it smell? Who joined you? What did you talk about?

Action suggestion

Cook and eat (slowly, reflectively) a big, scrumptious meal. Praise God, before, after, or during, with thanks for the taste, variety, texture, and smell of the foods.

Your thoughts

_____

_____

_____

_____

_____

_____

_____

_____

_____

_____

The Art of Storytelling

The Christian community lives within story, moves around its roomy chambers so often they become as familiar as home. We know that a mix of comic/tragic, hero/villain makes a good story. Without a family feud, Romeo and Juliet (or their modern counterparts in *West Side Story*) would have been merely another pair of love-struck, moony adolescents. Without Iago and his craftily planted seeds of jealousy, Othello and Desdemona would've celebrated a bland twenty-fifth anniversary with a tame reception at the Elks Club.

In the Hebrew-Christian tradition of story, sweet and sour, venom and blessing are just as dramatically intertwined. In fact, we greet Jezebel's murderous plots, Herod's slaughter of babies, and Jesus' miraculous cures with the same response: "The Word of the Lord." "Thanks be to God." Traitors, bigots, despots, prophets, widows, youth: all belong to God.

Long before we heard stories in church, we were snagged by the phrase, "Once upon a time...." The child begging "tell me a story" voices the universal human need for meaning. Stories can connect us to something greater, unguessed potential and larger possibilities. They link us not only with our own truths, but also with those of people far different than we. The story puts us in touch with the basic humanness beneath our differences.

For instance, I may never have lost a beloved sister. Yet if I have wept at Beth's death in *Little Women*, I have had the experience through another. I may not know what it means to lose a spouse. Yet C.S. Lewis recounts his wife's death in *A Grief Observed* so clearly that I can participate. Their story has been popularized in the poignant book and movie, *Shadowlands*.

Stories shape our world views, reinforcing or challenging what we think is true. Furthermore, stories carry our memories, both personal and collective. We may forget the exact dates of the Holocaust, but Elie Wiesel's stories of it are unforgettable. *Hotel Rwanda* brought the genocide of a distant country into the homes and theaters of North Americans with startling directness. Seeing what one family endured gave faces and concrete details to the news reports. The story showed us the human toll of the tragedy more vividly than any other medium could.

While human tribes may no longer gather around the campfire for bedtime legends, we still love stories. The only difference is that now they may be told through television or movies. For one attuned to the art of faith, they convey powerful messages about God.

Isak Dinesen, author of *Out of Africa*, says, "Any sorrow can be borne if a story can be told about it." Recounting the Vacation that Went Awry, a family proudly recounts its triumph over adversity. If we can laugh at dire circumstances, we deflate their power and change them to comedy.

We're all taught to "love our neighbor" but a good author or storyteller shows us how to love even the worst thug. The creator of a character knows exactly which detail will help us empathize with the ax murderer, the boozy residents of *Cannery Row*, or Anna

Karenina, the adulteress. Such fine creation surely follows the model of a God who loved David the adulterer, Peter the betrayer, and Thomas the doubter with equal audacity.

In the Old Testament, faith was handed down through stories. While a fact is one-dimensional, a story is open-ended and multi-layered. We can all be grateful that when he taught us how to live, Jesus didn't roll out a list of rules. He knew a better way to connect us to truth, each other, and God. So he began, "A certain man was traveling from Jerusalem to Jericho…" or many other variations on "Once upon a time." When he tried to explain his identity, he didn't reach for theological abstractions. He used the power of metaphor: vine and branches, living water, bread of life. He didn't write a dissertation on human suffering; he ended his time on earth like every other human being, and died a particularly brutal death at that.

The genius in storytelling is not only the concrete detail that brings the person alive, but the material that's omitted. What happened to the prodigal son after the welcome home party? How did Lazarus' second death compare with the first? Did Pontius Pilate or Herod suffer from sleeplessness or guilt? How did Mary Magdalene exercise leadership in the early church? Ah, that's where our imaginations, stimulated by story, come into play.

RELEVANT QUOTES

The story begins when the telling stops.

God made humans because God loves a story.

—WILLIAM BAUSCH

POEM

GIFT WRAP WITH THUNDER AND CADENCE, PLEASE

To anyone else, I'd give a gift.
To him, I'd tell a story.

He'd unwrap each word
and fold the paper,
cradle his passport to that country,
name its trees,
and shake the hero's hand.

Then he'd draw its lineage,
arrange it in the repertoire.
Not for display:
legends wither in a case.

When tones of boy colored the man's voice,
I'd take the grandma role
bringing the silent child
a basket woven of words.
Spell broken, son ransomed.
Patriarchs may shout, but grannies signal.

PAUSE TO REFLECT

- Do you nourish your soul with good reading, as you'd feed your body good food? What stories and films are your favorites?

- At Christmas, what stories were you told as a child? Which ones do you tell your children or grandchildren?

ACTION SUGGESTION

Visit the bookstore or library this week. Find your favorite books and re-read them, or find some new favorites. Enjoy.

River, Mountain, Sea

God's artistry creates spectacular settings where humans create their own works of art. God who made both human beings and natural wonders must've seen the harmonies between humanity and the places where we live. If we observe closely, we learn much about our creator from the natural world.

RIVER

Sometimes we move in a clear direction, toward a goal. We channel our energies and abilities to one special end and exult when we achieve it. Anyone who has finished a quilt, a marathon, a book, or a demanding project knows the triumph of accomplishment.

At such times, we might understand the symbol of a river for God. We are caught up in its flow, washed by its waters, tiny drops united in one surge, a shining, silvery path in sun. We feel confident we can tap this power no matter what obstacle we face.

PAUSE TO REFLECT

Imagine a mighty river flowing through broad green banks, sequined in the sun. Hear its swirling music and drumming tempo, feel the silky coolness of its waters, the light spray in your face. Feel yourself flowing with its force. Don't worry about drowning because this is an imaginary river. Give yourself over to floating without strain, carried in its strong current. Remember being a child, when a body of water represented play, freedom from clothes and indoor constraints, the juicy pleasure of an afternoon without clocks.

Now take it a step further. Imagine the river as God and yourself as part of the river.

- What do you want to say to this God of whom you are so much a part?
- What do you want to do, empowered by the force of this God?
- What do you want to give God?
- What must you let go of to sink completely into God's "height and depth, width and breadth"?

Pause to reflect

- Have you ever felt like you were placed squarely in the stream of God's goodness, like a boat in a river? What happened to place you there? Could you repeat that experience, or was it surprising gift?

Mountain

Sometimes we are supremely happy, drawing on blessing and living out of gratitude. It takes a major upheaval to shake our grounded conviction that we are God's child, living in the circle of God's care. We know ourselves as part of a larger story that stretches before our birth and after our death. We realize how trivial our concerns are in the grander scheme.

At such times, we relate to the mystery of the mountains. It is no accident that throughout Scripture, the mountaintop is a privileged place for meeting God. Endless waves receding toward the horizon are covered in more evergreens than anyone could count.

The stillness of forests is broken only by a bird's call or the wordless song of a stream.

The vastness of the landscape does two things. It dwarves us so we see human affairs as small in the larger scheme. Trivial concerns wash away as we stand in awe of God's majesty. Then we live and move within the hands of a God far greater than we could dream.

PAUSE TO REFLECT

- Picture yourself in a mountain forest. Smell the pine needles, glistening after a rain. Walk on soft loam past aspen and fir. Hike to a peak and look down. Between you and the horizon stretch more mountaintops, some glazed with snow, others polished granite in the sun. Tired from the climb, you sit and relax; your thoughts drift toward the creator of this scene.

- Imagine God creating the mountains. Did God scoop and carve, scrunch and seed? God formed mountaintops looking delicate as meringues, even though they were shaped from stone. To clothe the granite hills, God created an ecology that would take humans hundreds of years to study. In that life cycle, God created a model for human life: birth, death, rebirth.

SEA

No one could calculate God's love, any more than they could add up the number of water drops in the ocean. Maybe that's why the sea has always symbolized infinity. For many people, it still represents the abundance of God's love. The message of its creator is, "Look how outrageously I love you. You could no more lose my love than you could stop the rolling of waves into shore." Those who spend time on the beach relax into a sense of blessing, forgetting their usual worries.

The sea contains myriad colors: green, shading to aqua, shading to violet, shading to deep navy-purple. Seasoned sailors can read the depth by the color. And what could be more spectacular than waves dashing rocks? For sheer pizzazz, it rivals a child delighting in a wild, free *splat*.

Of course, the sea can wreak the havoc of a tsunami or Hurricane Katrina. Again, the dark and the light clash. The symbol of sea encompasses both polarities. The beautiful turns destructive. Clearly, God's designs here are beyond simple human equations of good and bad, right and wrong.

SCRIPTURE

Jesus, too, had profound experiences with rivers, mountains, and sea. For him, as well as for us, there was a link between inner and outer landscapes. Read the accounts of his baptism in the Jordan (Mark 1:9–11), his transfiguration on a high mountain (Matthew 17:1–9), his walking on the sea of Galilee (Matthew 14:22–33).

RELEVANT QUOTES

In fierce landscapes, one knows that "being good, being sweet, being nice will not cause life to sing."
—BELDEN LANE, QUOTING CLARISSA PINKOLA ESTES

…it is only a little planet
But how beautiful it is.
—ROBINSON JEFFERS

PAUSE TO REFLECT

- Of the three natural elements in this step—river, mountain, sea—which one is for you the clearest expression of God's creative life? If something else speaks better to you, what is it? Why?

step 32

The Art of Graceful Aging

When I was a child, grandmothers wore black "old lady shoes" and spent a lot of time in rocking chairs. Today, grandmothers jet off to Sri Lanka to do business consulting, run marathons, model clothing, lead yoga classes, ride bikes through Tuscany, and organize corporations. The transition from one generation to the next is enough to give anyone the bends. But I'm grateful for vibrant role models who have turned aging into an art.

We have always known that borderlands are rich territories where interesting things happen. When the gospels cue us that Jesus walks the edges of Tyre and Sidon, we know something dramatic will occur. When different ethnic groups meet, there's a lively diversity that's missing from the bland sameness of homogeneity. Biodiversity is greatest where different habitats meet. Teaching and learning become more exciting when different disciplines come together. (And so, we hope, art and faith enrich each other.)

If this is true on a natural plane, how much more so when we approach the border between this life and the next. Then we can see who we have become on earth, and what we will carry into heaven. Just as each phase of life brought out different facets of the person, so the final one enables many to look back over their life's artwork, enjoy the fullness of the picture, perhaps do one last revision.

There are some qualifiers, of course. Not everyone has the health or income to remain lively, successful, and gorgeous into their eighties. Advertising has presented air-brushed fictions of the elderly, who look like they're forty-five and apparently do nothing but take cruises and play golf. We know the sad realities of fixed incomes, poor health, and elder abuse—to say nothing of exhaustion! But we've also learned from older people that the physical isn't the ultimate definition of the human being.

We see in many older people an enviable wisdom, a calm flexibility which can be won only through long experience. They relax when the grandchildren act up in church in a way they never did when their own offspring were racing matchbox cars down the pews. They have the freedom to say whatever they please, and don't press the conversational "edit" button out of fear. (For example, the grannies who rage against war, the Mothers of the Disappeared, and the protesters who cross the line for a just cause.) Their faith has survived numerous crises and emerged strong. They know what's important, and have little time or energy to waste on fluff. Because they have endured roller-coastery trips, they give us hope.

Older people model how to gather our memories and find what is sacred within them. What's clear at a distance was often murky in the moment; age can bring perspective. It takes a full lifetime to see how God was present in downturns and ascents, and how all the pieces fit together.

Foremothers and fathers in the faith have always modeled for the young, living witnesses to the fact that over the long haul God can be trusted. Sarah's laughter spills joyfully across the Old Testament; she and Abraham chuckle as they push a baby carriage through the retirement home.

As with any of the arts, bitter and sweet blend as we approach death. We can be grateful to those who are dying and try to articulate it for those of us who will follow. During a concert at the National Pastoral Musicians convention in Cincinnati, July 2003, composer David Haas gave some background on a dying friend for whom he wrote the song "Take Me Home." When David went to visit, his friend spoke in sublime understatement. "I've got good news and bad news," he said. "The bad news is, I don't feel so hot. The good news is, Christ reigns."

RELEVANT QUOTES

If it's half as good as the half we've known,
then here's to the rest of the road! —A DRINKING SONG

As we grow old…the beauty steals inward.

—RALPH WALDO EMERSON

Aging is not "lost youth," but a new stage of opportunity and strength. —BETTY FRIEDAN

When you have loved as she has loved, you grow old beautifully.

—W. SOMERSET MAUGHAM

The longer I live the more beautiful life becomes.

—FRANK LLOYD WRIGHT

I never feel age….If you have creative work, you don't have age or time. —LOUISE NEVELSON

POEM

As a young man, Archbishop Lamy made the radical decision to leave his native Clermont, France, and become a missionary to the southwestern United States. His struggles and achievements are recounted in Willa Cather's novel *Death Comes for the Archbishop*. His home and garden can still be seen at Bishop's Lodge, a resort near Santa Fe, New Mexico. This poem imagines him looking back on a full life, well lived.

THE ARCHBISHOP'S APRICOTS

Warm resin of afternoon light
glazes the tawny cathedral face;
Sisters of Loreto settled snug in
the Sainte Chapelle of Santa Fe.

At last Archbishop Lamy, wearing a
floppy hat, can putter in his garden,
touch the hard green nub of apricot,
its tiny swollen seam.

Round adobe frames the azure sky, burning
above his patch of France: lilacs, acacias,
orchards, wines, white chapel of boyhood
closer now than recent Comanche raids.

Georgia O'Keeffe sculpts a perfect spiral
long after Lamy lives it: he distills, prunes
and harvests memories. The lavish garden
flourishes, like himself, on foreign soil.

The ground of exile flowers beneath the mesas
and pillars of vast sky; he builds with stone
the shades of native Clermont. The last days
swell like bud: "I shall die of having lived."

The Art of Yoga

During Mass, Catholics make a confession of sin to God. I sometimes feel like I should say it to my body. Day after day, I pour the toxins into it: tension, unhealthy food, sometimes alcohol. And day after day, it plugs along, uncomplaining. It will speak now and then with a skin cancer or a sore tooth, an achy back or a bout of flu. Sometimes it even shouts, with sleeplessness or weight loss, what the mind denies: "Too much stress!" It contradicts the "I'm doing just fine, thanks" message by broadcasting, "Pay attention to me!" By and large, it is a humble servant, an overlooked ally too often abused.

Sadly, I know what it loves: exercise, fruits and vegetables, massage, sun screen, rest. But I don't always provide the basics. For too many years, Catholic education focused on the soul. Good students, we became "heady," overlooking the marvelous harmony of body and spirit.

When the two come together, that juncture is sacrament. For instance, when we receive the Eucharist, we taste bread, believing it feeds our souls. The physical and the mental join hands in the dance. Neither can serve God without the other. The "disembodied" person tries—but how sad to not communicate with someone as close as our own bodies!

One of the few times I listen to my body is during a yoga class. That pause in a rushed routine doesn't come often enough, and I'm not an expert. But my amateurism helps me understand others who have neglected this helpful resource.

For those of us who live in our heads, dragging the body around like clunky chariots, yoga is a huge step toward integration. The first basic stretch reveals a deposit of achy tension in sore muscles. Over time, the neglected body responds to different poses with a strength, flexibility, and grace we never dreamt we had.

Most yoga teachers focus on the miracle of breath. Precious oxygen feathers through our systems, keeping us alive when we are unconscious of it. The only time we notice the respiratory system is when it goes out of whack: a cold, an airless space, pneumonia.

Far from being an expert in world religions, I nevertheless appreciate the correspondence between Jesus' teaching and the wisdom of this ancient Eastern practice. "Wherever two or more are gathered in my name, there am I in the midst of them," he said. The Sanskrit word *satsang* names a similar group: a truth-company, or a community of the wise. "None of us is as smart as all of us," the popular saying goes. We may have felt the strength of the community at a rally to restrict gun violence or end war. We may have gotten goosebumps as we sang "We Shall Overcome" together. Or perhaps a liturgy with a lively assembly touched us in a way few others have. In a workshop or prayer group, we felt the synergy of fellow pilgrims. We arrived at insights we might never have grasped alone.

So too when people practice yoga together, a rich silence descends. Most groups are remarkably forgiving of klutzy newcomers. Eventually we learn to avoid comparisons and to stretch toward the marvelous flexibility the body is capable of. By the final greeting, *Namaste*, or "the God in me greets the God in you," we feel a surprising kinship with class members. Like members of Alcoholics Anonymous or Weight Watchers, we're all in this together.

POEM

YOGA

My arms the pagoda
that greets the dawn
frames the eastern sky
encloses the menagerie.

Cobra and crocodile,
dog and rabbit,
all coil within,
all duly reverenced.

My warrior may wobble
but my tree stands tall, rooted in
earth. Arms and legs stretch to star.
A peaceful bow, a blessing. Namaste.

RELEVANT QUOTES

Yoga is to everlastingly dance the dance of deities.

—KOFI BUSIA

Yoga calms the fluctuations of the mind. —PATANJALI

ACTION SUGGESTIONS

Write a dialogue with your body. What does it tell you? What do
you say to it? If you feel distant from your body, create a rite of reconciliation with it.

Try a yoga class or get a video and follow it. It may be awkward
at first, but you may develop a liking for it over time.

The Art of Teaching

Jesus told the crowds all these things in parables; without a parable he told them nothing. This was to fulfill what had been spoken through the prophet:

> *I will open my mouth to speak in parables;*
> *I will proclaim what has been hidden from the foundation of the world.* MATTHEW 13:34–35

Somewhere along the line, most people had a good teacher. Maybe not a great teacher, but at least one they remember fondly. Draw on that memory now, as we explore what it means to make teaching an art.

Artful teaching isn't a dull, heavy-handed way to pass on information. When the class wants to run from the room, screaming with boredom, we sometimes blame them. Yet the responsibility to make teaching engaging and creative rests with the teacher.

Some do it admirably: they are the Michelangelos of teaching. We read or hear about them in the news when they win awards, and envy those in their classes. But we also know unsung teachers, who show up in all kinds of weather, seek the most creative way to convey their content, and rarely get applause. This step asks, "What makes them tick? How can our own teaching be more like theirs?"

All readers of this book may not be professional teachers or catechists. Yet most people teach in some way. Maybe it means training the new person on the job, or influencing another generation. Maybe the audience is nieces, nephews, or the neighbor's kids. In some way, even unconsciously, most of us pass on what we feel is most important.

Marshall McLuhan once said, "The medium is the message." That means focusing not only on the content we're teaching, but on how we're putting it across. Many of us have suffered through deadly lectures. But we understand now that lecturing may not be the best method—for adult learners or for anyone. People tune out brain-numbing talk or writing; they learn from story or activity.

When the overblown controversy erupted over *The Da Vinci Code*, it showed how art can teach. Suddenly, interest in classical art like "The Last Supper" soared. People with little interest in theology were caught up in story.

Joseph Arner, writing a letter to the editors of *America* magazine (July 31, 2006, 37–38), argues that the church should not so flippantly dismiss the success of the best-selling novel. Instead, it should look like a parent at a child, seeing the need and how this book meets it. A person's desire to be involved in another's story is natural and human. Arner concludes,

> There is much to be learned from the phenomena surrounding *The Da Vinci Code*. One is that the world very often does not listen to historically accurate doctrinal explanations. It listens to stories that are rich in true and human intangibles. It yearns for the truth of fiction and parable, rather than the truth of catechesis and history. And the church should listen and learn before it thinks of itself as so mature, losing its members to popular trends because it no longer speaks the world's language.

The Da Vinci Code blip on the radar will vanish when the next best-seller hits the bookstores and movie screens, but what remains is the truth. To compete with modern media, good teachers must be artists.

What this means in tangible terms is that an elementary teacher doesn't produce a map of the world and instruct the children to memorize the countries and capitals. Instead, he or she and the children design passports, choose a country to visit, and then construct an African hut, surrounded by the proper vegetation. They learn to count to ten in Swahili and sample native foods. They sing African songs, beat the drums, see the art, and hear the folk tales.

A high school teacher doesn't lecture about the sweatshops of the industrial age; he gives the students an experience of one. Collating and stapling bundles of paper under time pressure, competing with other groups, they get the picture. Then they may turn to their textbooks to complete the message, but the learning engraved on their senses is more likely to remain.

Adults who found botany tedious in school are captivated by a tour of tidal pools, prairie grasslands, or coral reefs with an engaging guide. When they touch, smell, and observe the growth of natural wonders, they say, "Wow. I never knew all that was there." True learning such as this excites us; we can't get enough of it. Our minds are made to absorb wonder; the artful teacher understands this need and like a ham on the stage, plays to it.

How does this affect the field of religious education? One solution might be to turn to the long Christian history of teaching the faith through the arts. Much is available online or through the library; many cities offer free or discounted concerts, theater, and museum hours to students. Previous steps have already referred to the persuasiveness of beauty, the enchantment of story, visual arts, and song.

The mystery of the arts can nourish the soul, points out Cardinal Godfried Danneels: "I ask myself whether we are using sufficiently one of the doors that leads to God—the door named Beauty." For contemporary people, beauty is disarming and irresistible. He adds another dimension: the "saints who shone with beauty." ("The Contemporary Person and the Church," *America*, July 30, 2001, 9).

RELEVANT QUOTES

Teachers open the door. You enter by yourself.

—CHINESE PROVERB

Good teaching is one-fourth preparation and three-fourths theater.

—GAIL GODWIN

PAUSE TO REFLECT

- Remember the best teacher you ever had. What did you learn from this person? What do you think made him or her tick? Was the teaching an art form? Why or why not?

- Imagine a class sitting in front of you. You're a guest teacher in a series titled "The Most Important Thing I Want to Pass On." Today it's your turn. What do you want to say? How will you teach it?

ACTION SUGGESTION

Write a note, phone, or e-mail someone you'd consider a fine teacher. Thank them for what they've taught.

The Art of Friendship

She phones and her voice arcs over the last fifty years. We were friends in kindergarten and remain friends now that she's the grandmother of three. I can hear the concern in her voice. A geriatric nurse, she helped my father through aging and mourned with me when he died. We've shared some trials and still connect.

We laugh as loudly as we did in grade school with her granddaughter who hasn't quite mastered the "L" sound. Viewing twenty-five women assembled for our fortieth high school reunion, the grandchild commented, "Wotsa wadies!" (The same child, told how various grandparents would arrive for the birth of her first sibling, and how long they would stay to help, listened carefully. Then she asked, "When will the baby leave?")

Even though we live in different cities a long plane ride apart, we relate in ways that newer friends do not. We have the same long lines connecting to our parents, our early schools, our high school crushes—or lack of dates. She was beautiful at eighteen; she remains beautiful at fifty-eight. Though I see her only once or twice a year, she holds a firm place in my heart. Her phone call delays me a bit, but I wouldn't cut it short. I walk into exercise class late but proud to have such a cherished friend.

A second friend swore she had "no particular talents." Alison envied people who excelled at interior design, engineering, painting, teaching, nursing, or baking. She'd wonder what her unique gift was as she explored different areas that never quite seemed to click. Then she became critically ill with a rare cancer. The response revealed a special gift she'd never recognized: nurturing friendships.

A network of people helped in many ways. Some drove to doctor appointments, others cooked, others sent funny cards, some planted, watered, and weeded her garden, one arranged a hot air balloon ride to celebrate the last chemotherapy treatment. One sent a gift certificate for a restaurant; another found the softest cotton pajamas for the hospital. Two runners signed up for a marathon Race for the Cure in Alison's honor. One group met regularly to pray for the success of her treatment.

Alison found the outpouring of affection humbling, but several people pointed out, "It's what you've always done for others. It's coming back to you now." No one had endured the cancer ordeal with more support. The final word isn't in yet, but if, as some doctors believe, the patient's attitude makes a difference, Alison will heal. And she'll never again wonder about her special gift.

A third friend, Sister Maria, has made friendship such an art that people gravitate to her kitchen and her support. She stages an annual squirt gun contest for the neighbors' kids, faithfully attends the performances, graduations, and weddings of other friends' children, and helps raise three young children whose mother died unexpectedly. Bewildered by their loss, they know only that she will have them for slumber parties, providing cupcakes and trips to the local water park. A sympathy card wouldn't do it. Sister gives her time and energy instead.

People like Alison and Sister Maria seem to know exactly what a friend needs at exactly the right time. (They may have honed this knowledge through a few mistakes—but what novelist doesn't revise endlessly?) Then they follow through. So if a movie or concert that Mandy would love comes to town, they don't just muse, "Mandy might like that…." Nope. They call her up, buy tickets, and arrive on her doorstep ready to go.

Some artful touches aren't that time-consuming. How long does it take to forward an e-mail joke? Other needs are infrequent. Under that heading might come commiserating after a divorce, diagnosis, break-up, traffic ticket, or job loss. The true friend knows that pieties won't cut it then. One friend needs the presence of the other, no matter how long it takes.

Sometimes we just need someone who'll bumble through with us—whether it's setting up the Christmas tree or cleaning out the swamp cooler. If we're fortunate, our friends have "been there, done that"—whether it's buying a car, negotiating a sticky situation at work, or surviving a teenager. Somehow, they manage to share their expertise without being condescending. Because of them, we know a little what it means to be friends with God.

SCRIPTURE

"I do not call you servants any longer, because the servant does not know what the master is doing; but I have called you friends" (John 15:15). When Jesus said this to his disciples at the last supper, they were accustomed to thinking of the deity as distant and probably punitive. What must it have meant to them that God-become-human shared their storytelling, boating, washing, eating, walking, laughing, complaining—each day's most ordinary experiences?

What was true for the first disciples is also true for us. When Jesus says he is your friend, what does it mean in the context of your ordinary days?

PAUSE TO REFLECT

- Savor the memory of a friend. What have you or the other person done to maintain the relationship? In what ways have you made it an art?

RELEVANT QUOTES

I tell you the more I think, the more I feel that there is nothing more truly artistic than to love people.

—VINCENT VAN GOGH

It's a drum and arms waving,
It's a bonfire at midnight on the top edge of a hill,
this meeting again with you.

—RUMI

ACTION SUGGESTION

Divide a piece of paper or a page on your computer screen into two columns. In the first column, list your friends. In the second, list exactly what they might need from you right now. Avoid abstractions like "care." Use specifics like, "lunch next week," "a call tonight," or "a donut and a walk in the park Saturday morning." Then do one thing on the list every week for the next month.

YOUR THOUGHTS

_____

_____

_____

_____

_____

_____

_____

From Aqua to Azure: The Art of Snorkeling

O Lord, how manifold are your works!
In wisdom you have made them all....
Yonder is the sea, great and wide,
creeping things innumerable are there,
living things both small and great.
There go the ships,
and Leviathan that you formed to sport in it. PSALM 104:24–26

An oddly-dressed bunch of people prepares to jump off a boat in the Atlantic Ocean: wearing wet suits, masks, and breathing tubes, lurching awkwardly with long black fins on their feet. This clumsy and unlikely crowd has been mysteriously chosen for a rare treat.

This odd-looking bunch of snorkelers has the chance to view a part of God's creation never seen by most humans. They have come to John Pennekamp Coral Reef State Park near Key Largo, Florida, to rest their faces and float their bodies on the Atlantic Ocean. What transpires next, they cannot forget. Snorkeling can be the artful experience poet Christopher Fry describes:

The enterprise

Is exploration into God.

In ordinary life ashore, we get brief glimpses into God, experience our small patches of paradise. But here the work of a vivid creator surprises and delights especially because it is so rarely seen. The boat captain can expertly read the outline of the reef in jade tones against darker navy blue. We anchor at Sea Gardens, a stretch of the only living coral reef in the continental U.S.

It is well named. The coral flowers here in intricate textures and shapes. Anemones sway to waves which rock fish, humans, and plants in the same cradle to the same rhythm. As huge, lacy purple fronds float, their structure of tiny interlocking channels echoes the network of veins in the human body or the silhouette of bare tree branches and twigs against a salmon-tinged sunset.

Caught up in a school of silvery fish or coming almost face to face with a yellow and black striped angelfish, the human visitor feels part of their world, suddenly conscious of the ninety percent water that constitutes the body. The colors dazzle: dark blue with neon orange spots, the mosaic of green, gold, and blue flashing on the clownfish. Emerald glints on the surface of a giant clam; its deep inner pool opens to reveal a mother of pearl sheen. Barracudas and giant tortoises drift happily past paddling tourists.

It is a time out of time, the clock forgotten as one becomes a giant eye absorbed in wonder, intent on the play of light over every glistening detail. One of the hardest lessons to learn is trust. Yet here the visitor sees "God in the details" as well as the big picture. If such concrete care is lavished on delicate coral which can take years to grow an inch, what of us, we of little faith?

While we are absorbed in wonder, we forget bad news and unpaid bills. We become what God must have originally meant us to be: made for delight. If we were to fill out a comment card on creation now, we could write only one word: wow.

When we clamber ashore, what do we carry besides fins and masks?

Surely the memory of teeming, colorful life: what Christ brought us in abundance. We are willing to rest in God's mercy as in an ocean. Surely the creator of this stunning blue world gives no less attention to us, beloved children.

Ashore we'll meet the four Ds: disputes, disease, despair and death. But we may bear them with more serenity, more confidence. The crisis passes and the divine care endures. After all, God's watery design has outlasted human war and disaster. This world floats beyond our screaming headlines. It has a steady permanence that underlies the painful shocks, an artistic vision broader than what we might immediately see. Because Christ reigns, all will eventually be redeemed, restored, re-created. Snorkeling isn't Sunday liturgy—but it sends some of the same uplifting messages.

Walking ashore seems clumsy after the easy drifting on water. It is a grace to be, even in our klutzy way, amphibian, able to move between worlds. Without such experiences of beauty, religion might be a pale and empty thing. *With* such experiences, we can live out of a pool, perhaps an ocean, of joy. Although we live on land, we never leave the ocean; the ocean is within.

ACTION SUGGESTION

Visit an aquarium, rent a DVD, or get a book from the library about the world underwater. Enjoy the pictures; marvel at God's creativity.

The Inner Drama of the Gospels

We've seen drama before: a movie with special effects, a high school performance of *Our Town* that left the audience misty-eyed, a local theater that produced rollicking comedy, or an outdoor Shakespeare-fest that brought the bard alive. All are art forms that can inspire, sadden, challenge, frighten, bring laughter, prompt discussion.

But they don't hold a candle to the inner dramas that play out in most lives. We rehearse and rehash conversations, work through conflicts, prepare or analyze actions, plan the future, savor the present, and remember the past. People smile when they catch us talking to ourselves—if they knew what was going on inside, they might buy tickets!

This step explores another dimension of the inner drama. Authors like John Sanford have suggested that the different characters in a Bible story can all represent different facets of ourselves. So, for instance, we are both Martha and Mary, sometimes driven by need to furious action; at other times, restful, serene, and contemplative. We can also be both the prodigal son and his brother. Sometimes we're

137

playful; sometimes overly responsible. On better days, we give the generous welcome the boys' father offered them both.

On a day when I was scheduled for nasty dental surgery, the reading was Matthew 14:22–33, the story of Jesus walking on water. Jesus has sent his friends on ahead of him and remains ashore to pray. Meanwhile on the sea, the disciples' boat is battered by waves. Early in the morning, Jesus walks to it across water. Terrified, the disciples call out, "It's a ghost!" Despite Jesus' reassurance, Peter proposes a test: "If it is you, Lord, command me to walk across the water." Jesus invites him with one word: "Come."

Most of us know the rest of the story: Peter starts out bravely but becomes frightened when he sees what he's doing. When he calls out in fear, Jesus grabs his hand and asks, "Why did you doubt?" As they climb back into the boat, the storm calms and the seafarers worship Jesus.

Because I was somewhat apprehensive that day, I first identified with Peter, flailing on the water's surface. When Jesus asked, "Why did you doubt?" I could string out answers, but they would all poof like smoke in his face. The litany of times I've doubted would fill this book, the crises were eventually resolved, yet still I lack trust. Like Peter, I imagine terrible possibilities swirling in the seas beneath bare feet.

My parental side identifies with Jesus who reaches out his hand immediately. If your child is drowning, you don't begin with a lecture about why he or she shouldn't have been swimming in the deep end without a floatie. You save first, scold later.

Back to Peter and his friends. I want to cling to Jesus' hand in the storms. Most of us are surrounded by the choppy waves of relationships, stress, job crises, health and financial worries. When Jesus calms the inner storms, we want to worship him in gratitude. I conclude by making a mantra of his words, to repeat on the way to surgery and the next challenge I'll face: "Take heart. It is I. Fear not."

In *Walking on Water,* Madeleine L' Engle sees Peter as remembering for one brief, glorious moment how to walk across the lake. He "strode with ease," the way he was meant to, then forgot. But because he called for help, he didn't drown. She believes that "the impossible still happens to us" when we let down the barriers we've built. She concludes: "It is one of those impossibilities I believe in; and in believing, my own feet touch the surface of the lake, and I go to meet him, like Peter, walking on water" (196–197).

Pause to reflect

Let's take for an example of this approach to Scripture a gospel story: the cure of Jairus' daughter (Mark 5:21–24, 35–43; Luke 8:40–42, 49–56). The characters with speaking parts are Jairus, the child's father, Jesus, the messengers from Jairus' house who tell him his daughter has died, and the paid mourners who wail and weep.

After reading the story, try to identify these folks with your inner voices. When are you the prayerful parent, convinced that Jesus can do anything, no matter how absurd it may seem? When do you speak with the healing authority of Jesus, confident that God wants to restore full health to all God's creatures? When do you focus on the bad news? When do you cry because you don't know what else to do?

The climax of the drama occurs when Jesus says, "Child, get up!" When do you invite your inner child to come forth with that gentle welcome? When do you honor that part of yourself that wants to play, delight in creation, watch clouds, stargaze, or take a nap? The heroine of the play doesn't speak. When are you as sound asleep as the little girl? Knowing that he will understand your deepest self without words, what help do you need from Jesus now?

SCRIPTURE

These passages might lend themselves to identifying yourself with the different characters. Try one: Jesus Heals the Centurion's Servant (Matthew 8:5–13), Jesus and the Samaritan Woman (John 4:1–42), Jesus Heals a Paralytic (Luke 5:17–26), Jesus Is Anointed (John 12:1–8).

PAUSE TO REFLECT

- When you try this approach to Scripture, identifying characters with your own inner voices, how does it work for you?

YOUR THOUGHTS

_____

_____

_____

_____

_____

_____

_____

_____

_____

_____

The Art of Appreciation

This letter comes often to newspaper advice columnists: "I spent time and money on a wedding present. The couple never thanked me!" or "I always send my grandson a card and gift on his birthday. Why doesn't he respond?" Answers may vary, but in the latter case Dear Abby recommends calling the grandson's bluff. "I bet you'll hear from him if you quit sending it!" she chortles.

We're lucky that Abby's advice doesn't apply to our relationship with God. What if God, like the sad grandparent, cut us off because we didn't acknowledge the gifts? It would be perfectly understandable. God places us in a beautiful world, showers us with blessings, and often gives us our heart's delight. We respond by worrying about what we don't have, ignoring what we have, and longing for more.

We might all be happier if we made appreciation into a fine art. In fact, we might begin to suspect we're rich in intangible wealth. What does it mean, for example, to have good health? No one knows until they've been sick. The return of energy, of interest in food and other people and work and life is a special resurrection.

Or what is the cost of security? Only those who have lived through a war can answer, knowing how it feels to sleep in quiet peace without fear.

The litany continues through natural wonders, human relationships, education, medical care, and housing. These examples of gratitude tie directly to the art of faith. One line from John's gospel is telling: "He spoke these words in the treasury of the temple" (8:20). It comes at the end of the passage where Jesus told the people, "I am the light of the world."

Let's play with these words a bit. The treasure room for any of us must be the heart and center of the home. Teresa of Avila imagined people as magnificent castles. She led them through many rooms before coming to the central core, where God abides, the source of light for the whole house. In Scripture, the house stands for the self. What's in our treasure room? What do we hold most dear? Answering that question helps us live from a deep pool of thanks.

What is art if not the heart's cry of "thanks," in whatever medium a person is skilled? A photographer who spends hours getting the exact slant of light on redwoods or apple blossoms, then takes the shot seventy-five times to get it perfect, must have a keen appreciation for the subject. A writer hones a text through endless revision because he or she loves the topic. Why would anyone spend the time on artwork if he or she didn't?

Luke's account of the last supper repeats a key phrase: "Then [Jesus] took a cup, and after giving thanks he said, 'Take this and divide it among yourselves'....Then he took a loaf of bread, and when he had given thanks, he broke it and gave it to them, saying, 'This is my body, which is given for you. Do this in remembrance of me'" (22:17, 19).

Even those who gather daily or weekly for Eucharist (which means "giving thanks") miss the point if the celebration isn't set within a thankful life. We have so much to be grateful for, it overflows the narrow confines of an hour. We also know that the ritual holds little meaning if it doesn't change our lives. Judas, after all, left the last supper and walked straight into betraying Jesus.

If anyone needs a visual reminder of gratitude, think of the child who gets exactly what she wants for Christmas—or gets a snow day off school in January. Her body cannot contain her joy: she hops, twirls, jumps on sofas and beds. Can our hearts fill with thanks like hers?

Pause to reflect

What's the "treasure room" in your house?

a library with a fireplace?

a homey kitchen filled with good food smells?

a restful bedroom, away from noise?

a pastel nursery?

a porch with rocking chairs, overlooking a garden?

a workshop, home office, or studio where you create?

Visualize that room, wherever it is, now.

Now explore the treasure room of your heart. You may need to clear some clutter first, but imagine yourself resting there in God, perhaps with the people you love.

Action suggestion

Every night this week, list the three things you were most grateful for today. At the end of the week, pray gratefully over the list.

Relevant quotes

Gratitude is the most exquisite form of courtesy.

—Jacques Maritain

Silent gratitude isn't much use to anyone.

—Gertrude Stein

step 39

Quilts, Clothes, & the Art of Shelter

As many of you as were baptized into Christ have clothed yourself with Christ. GALATIANS 3:27

Because quilting means sewing together scraps of fabrics, it's like crafting a life. There's a swatch of grandma's flannel nightgown; here's a patch from Uncle Roy's denim overalls; this floral piece came from a bridesmaid's dress. In the same way, we show the marks of family and friends on our lives.

Furthermore, we often stitch together different influences, memories, and events. Some colors seem like an odd combination, but together they make the whole. So do our lives create a pattern which could not be different because it's a unique work of art. We can't appreciate each section when it stands alone. But in relation to the big picture it becomes beautiful and inevitable. A telling line ends John's account of sharing the loaves and fishes. "When they were satisfied, he told his disciples, 'Gather up the fragments left over, so that nothing may be lost'" (6:12).

For those of us who live fragmented lives and divide our time among many commitments, that line is heartening. It means that to Jesus every little piece counts. Nothing, no matter how small, is wasted or unimportant. So too the quilter sees value in the slightest scrap: placing the coral fabric beside the azure one will make the total effect pop.

A FAMILY AFFAIR

The Grand Opening of the Rocky Creek Clothing Store was a family affair. The owner, a young woman named Zoe who had graduated from college in Hawaii, had a flair for clothing. She opened her own store on a quaint street of art galleries, restaurants, and antique shops. Her mother was the accountant. Her dad and uncle built the display shelves and designed a cozy fireplace. One aunt painted; another made curtains. Grandmothers and cousins cooked trays of food and her brother-in-law was the bartender. Her sister ordered a lei from Hawaii for Zoe to wear on opening day.

Customers delighted in the clothes and amused each other trying them on. Beautiful models strolled through the store wearing sweaters, jackets, and dresses that of course fit perfectly. The cash register rang steadily and door prizes added to the excitement.

Some might criticize this scene as a blatant exercise in retail therapy. But others might see another metaphor. Zoe's family was clothing her in affirmation and support. They knew the risk she had taken, the investment she'd made, the difficulty of predicting what would sell. Zoe was in turn helping her customers look beautiful.

LIVING BEAUTIFULLY

Some know the art of decorating. They can make a room or a home beautiful, often without much money. They know what colors go where, which furniture fits best. Sometimes they can't explain their style; they just go on instinct.

Those of us who don't have this knack are grateful to those who do. They can make a bedroom into a warm haven. After we've traveled all day, their talents make a hotel room seem like home. In a beautiful setting, our happiness soars and our spirits are revived. The decorator's art mirrors God's, who made the earth such a lovely home for humans.

SCRIPTURE

I will greatly rejoice in the Lord,
my whole being shall exult in my God;
for he has clothed me with the garments of salvation,
he has covered me with the robe of righteousness,
as a bridegroom decks himself with a garland,
and as a bride adorns herself with her jewels.
—ISAIAH 61:10

You shall be a crown of beauty in the hand of the Lord, and a royal diadem in the hand of your God. —ISAIAH 62:3

Consider the lilies of the field, how they grow; they neither toil nor spin, yet I tell you, even Solomon in all his glory was not clothed like one of these. But if God so clothes the grass of the field, which is alive today and tomorrow is thrown into the oven, will he not much more clothe you—you of little faith?
—MATTHEW 6:28–30

PAUSE TO REFLECT

Remember some piece of clothing you once wore, in which you knew you were "hot stuff." What does that feeling of looking great tell you about the deeper, spiritual meaning of clothing? How does God clothe us?

ACTION SUGGESTION

Clear out a closet or drawer. Give the stuff that won't fit to a charity. You might clothe someone else in beauty.

RELEVANT QUOTE

I want it fixed right because my quilts might go somewhere I ain't never going to go so they going to say, "This quilt made by Polly Bennett!" —"THE QUILTS OF GEE'S BEND"

YOUR THOUGHTS

_____

_____

_____

_____

_____

_____

_____

_____

_____

_____

_____

_____

Dayenu

An ancient Hebrew prayer, adapted

We close these reflections with words of praise. Knowing a little of God, learning how God, co-operating with us, makes our lives into artwork, we have cause for celebration. If only we had a brass band with jazz dancers to celebrate this ending and beginning. But we'll need something quieter here. We turn to an ancient way of honoring God and delighting in God's bounty. No matter how tough our circumstances seem to be, there is reason to rejoice. The Hebrews once prayed:

> If God had merely rescued us from Egypt, but not opened the sea for us…it would have been enough.

> If God had merely opened the sea for us but not supplied us with manna in the desert…it would have been enough.

> If God had only supplied us with manna in the desert, but not made a covenant with us…it would have been enough.

> If God had only made a convent with us but not given us the Sabbath…it would have been enough.

Followers of Jesus then Christianized the prayer:

> If God had only sent the Son and Jesus had not revealed to us a new gospel life, it would have been enough.

148

If Jesus had merely revealed a new gospel life and not suffered and died to show his love, it would have been enough.

If Jesus had only died for us to show his love and not risen from the dead, it would have been enough.

If Jesus had only risen from the dead and not sent his Spirit to guide the new community, it would have been enough.

If Jesus had only sent his Spirit to guide the new community and not given us the support of each other, it would have been enough.

We in turn pray:

If God had only given us life and not birthed us into a loving family, it would have been enough.

If God had only birthed us into a loving family and not given us the abilities to walk, think, and feel, it would have been enough.

If God had given us only the abilities to walk, talk, think, and feel and not given us a variety of other gifts as well, it would have been enough.

If God had given us only a variety of other gifts and not an education, it would have been enough.

If God had given us only an education and not the company of friends, it would have been enough.

If God had given us only the company of friends and not the wisdom of older guides, it would have been enough.

If God had given us only the wisdom of older guides and not the laughter of children, it would have been enough.

The form can be abbreviated somewhat:

If God had given us only sight and not hearing, it would have been enough.

If God had given us only hearing and not taste, it would have been enough.

If God had given us only taste and not touch, it would have been enough.

If God had given us only touch and not smell, it would have been enough.

If God had made eyes in only one color or hair in only one shade and not the endless varieties of tones and shapes, it would have been enough.

If God had given us only one body of water and not seven seas, countless lakes, and rivers, it would have been enough.

If God had hung only one star in heaven and not all the planets and a dazzling array of constellations, it would have been enough.

If God had painted only one sunrise or sunset and not sunrise and sunset daily, it would have been enough.

If God had made only one species of animal and not many kinds, it would have been enough.

If God had made only one flower and not a mind-boggling bouquet, it would have been enough.

If God had planted only one tree in Eden and not the forests which clothe the world in green, it would have been enough.

If God had given only one person the ability to create and play music and not countless musicians and composers, it would have been enough.

If God had inspired only one person to paint and not those who fill museums, galleries, studios, and homes with their paintings, it would have been enough.

If God had taught only one writer how to shape a plot and make the language sing and not enough writers to appeal to everyone's taste, it would have been enough.

If God had made only one color and not the rainbow of tones and textures we see daily, it would have been enough.

When we pray through our blessings this way, their staggering variety becomes abundantly clear—and almost overwhelming. If that is the case, focus on one or two a day, making up your own rhythms and specifics.

Pause to reflect

Adapt the "Dayenu" prayer to your own circumstances and setting. How do you feel, creating it?

Action suggestion

- Look back over the last forty days or steps. Write down three things you've learned about an artful life or God's artwork.

Your thoughts

_____

_____

_____

_____

_____

_____

_____

_____

_____

YOUR THOUGHTS